D0934339

Columbia University

Contributions to Education

Teachers College Series

No. 323

AMS PRESS

NEW YORK

THE SOLVING
OF PROBLEM-SITUATIONS
BY PRESCHOOL CHILDREN

AN ANALYSIS

BY

AUGUSTA ALPERT, Ph. D.

Teachers College, Columbia University
Contributions to Education, No. 323

Bureau of Publications
Teachers College, Columbia University
NEW YORK CITY
1928

216325

Library of Congress Cataloging in Publication Data

Alpert, Augusta, 1898–
    The solving of problem-situations by pre-school
children.

    Reprint of the 1928 ed., issued in series: Teachers
College, Columbia University. Contributions to
education, no. 323.
    Originally presented as the author's thesis,
Columbia.
    1. Child study. 2. Psychology, Comparative.
3. Apes. I. Title. II. Series: Columbia University.
Teachers College. Contributions to education, no. 323.
LB1117.A45 1972   155.4'23   74-176514
ISBN 0-404-55323-0

Reprinted by Special Arrangement with Teachers
College Press, New York, New York

From the edition of 1928 , New York
First AMS edition published in 1972
Manufactured in the United States

AMS PRESS, INC.
NEW YORK, N. Y.   10003

To N. H. and B. L.

ACKNOWLEDGMENTS

The writer wishes to acknowledge her indebtedness and gratitude to all those who have coöperated with her in the preparation of this study. She is especially grateful to Professors Ruth Andrus, R. S. Woodworth, and H. A. Ruger, the members of her dissertation committee at Columbia University, whose suggestions were as helpful as their interest was encouraging and stimulating. To the members of the staff at the Institute of Child Welfare Research she is grateful for their coöperation. No list of acknowledgments would be complete if it did not include the forty-four children at the Institute Nursery School who so cheerfully served as subjects and without whom this investigation could not have been undertaken or completed.

A. A.

CONTENTS

CHAPTER I

INTRODUCTION

STATEMENT OF PROBLEM

The "almost human" behavior, to use Yerkes'[1] phrase, of the chimpanzees which served as subjects for Köhler's experiments conducted at Tenerife and reported in his book, *The Mentality of Apes*,[2] suggested itself to the writer as an excellent starting point for a study of the solving behavior, and principally of the solving methods, of the preschool child when exposed to problem situations. Such a study constitutes the primary purpose of this investigation. The secondary purpose, a comparison between the solving behavior of children and that of apes, is subsidiary to the first and to that extent is the method or means of approach rather than the purpose or end of the investigation. In the strict sense of the term this cannot be regarded as a comparative study, for Köhler's experimentation was not specifically designed for this purpose. The writer, having to choose between adapting her technique to that of Köhler's and adapting it to the needs of the preschool children who served as subjects, naturally chose the latter. In the interest of further investigation along this line it was also deemed wise to follow a more highly controlled procedure.

In general, this difference in technique is in the direction of greater constancy in the objective details of the problem-situations as well as in the experimenter's approach toward the subjects. However, the nine problem-situations chosen for this investigation were made comparable as far as possible to those used by Köhler. Whatever changes were introduced will be indicated in the course of the following description.

SUBJECTS

Forty-four children attending the Nursery School of the Institute of Child Welfare Research, Teachers College, Columbia

[1] Yerkes, R. M., *Almost Human*. Century Publishing Co., 1925.

[2] Köhler, W., *The Mentality of Apes*. Harcourt, Brace & Co., 1925.

1

University, were used as subjects. They ranged in age from 19 to 49 months.

GENERAL DESCRIPTION OF TEST SITUATIONS

Series I

Situation A.—An attractive toy (balloon, duck, dog, doll, bird-on-ring, airplane, or string of beads) is suspended from the ceiling to within about 4 feet of the floor, by means of a red cord, such as is used for tying small parcels. The toy is out of the subject's reach. Five feet away, diagonally to the right of the suspended toy, is a green, hollow block 9 inches by 12 inches by 15 inches. This was taken from the roof equipment of the Nursery School attended by the subjects and was therefore a familiar object. The solution of the problem depends upon placing the block under the objective and using it as a footstool in reaching.

This test situation corresponds to the situation described by Köhler on page 40 of *The Mentality of Apes.* It will be noted that instead of bananas and oranges, which Köhler used, toys are substituted throughout the two Series; the block is the analogue of the box which Köhler provided; and the children were consistently tested individually so as to preclude imitation, competition, and other complications.

Situation B.—This differs from the previous situation only by the substitution of a small chair (such as is used in the playroom) for the hollow block, and corresponds to Köhler's substitution of a table and ladder for boxes, as described on page 49 of his book.

Situation C.—Here the objective is removed to a shelf 4 feet high, where it can be reached by means of the hollow block, now placed five feet to the left of the objective. Köhler commonly follows the practice of removing the objective to a different place, keeping other factors unchanged.

Situation D.—Here the setting of Situation A is reproduced except that the objective is hung higher so that it can be reached only by turning the block on the perpendicular side. This situation was not designed by Köhler but the device was hit upon by Sultan, the genius-ape, and by two of the other apes (see page 48 of *The Mentality of Apes*), and was therefore included in the Series.

Situation E.—In addition to the hollow block in its usual place, a wooden grocery box 12 inches by 15 inches by 18 inches is placed about 7 feet diagonally to the left of the objective, which is now hung still higher so that it can be reached only if the block is piled on top of the box and the structure mounted by the subject. The grocery box was introduced here instead of another block so as to provide a wide base upon which to place the upper block, thus insuring a stable structure and avoiding mishaps and fear of mishaps. The box was also taken from the nursery school equipment. This situation is described by Köhler on page 139 of his book.

Series II

Situation A.—The center of activity for this Series is a play-pen, 7½ feet long, 3 feet wide, and 2½ feet high, thus reaching to about the sternum of the subject. For this situation an attractive toy is placed outside the pen and the child is inside. Somewhat to his left lies an ordinary stick about a yard long. To procure the objective the subject must reach with the stick either through the bars or over the top of the pen. This situation is described by Köhler on page 32, the pen corresponding to the barred cage used in his experiment.

Situation B.—The setting remains the same except that a toy broom is substituted for the stick. Here again the substitution was introduced by the apes themselves, using tin drinking cups, straws, blankets, etc., in the absence of sticks. (See page 34 of *The Mentality of Apes.*)

Situation C.—The stick of Situation A is here placed outside the bars of the pen so that it can be reached only with the short stick (1 foot long) which lies inside the pen. The toy is placed as in Situation A but can be reached only with the long stick. The identical situation is used by Köhler and is described on page 180 of his study.

Situation D.—Two halves of a fishing rod are placed inside the pen. The toy is placed farther away so that it cannot be reached with either half. If the two halves are fitted at the metal ends, the joined stick is adequate to bridge the gap. Köhler uses ordinary bamboo sticks for this experiment, which is described on page 130 of his book.

GENERAL PROCEDURE

The subjects were always tested in the morning between nine and eleven, which meant taking the child from the playroom, roof, or yard, presumably to play another game.

The time spent in the testing-room varied from one and a half minutes to sixteen minutes, the usual time being about four to five minutes; only one subject stayed as long as sixteen minutes. The length of exposure to a situation was controlled by the experimenter's judgment, the determining factors being the interest of the subject, his activity, and the factor of fatigue. Time spent after interest had waned was found to be fruitless, for the subject would either turn his back on the field of action and amuse himself with his own devices or he would reach out for the objective in a mechanical, indifferent manner, quite obviously to satisfy the experimenter.

In some cases the experimenter found it advisable tô draw the experiment to a close even when the subject still manifested interest but engaged in just one response with complete absorption as though "wound up." Case 22 is illustrative and will be cited in a later section (page 21).

There were still other cases where interest seemed never to wane, yet it was deemed wise to terminate the experiment in order to avoid overstimulation of the subject. Thus it can be seen that the time spent in a situation depended upon the subject.

The experimenter fetched each child herself and usually chatted with him or her on the way to the testing-room. Upon entering, the subject was at once told what to do, though for the first Series this was hardly necessary since the situations were not only self-explanatory but even compelling, so that the subject would often "go after" the swinging objective of his own accord. The instructions, when necessary, were, "Do you see this dog (doll, bird, etc.)? See if you can get it." Or, "Yes, that's for you," in response to the subject's look of enquiry.

Each subject was given an opportunity on each of five different days to solve the first situation. After the first exposure it was rarely necessary to do more than swing the objective or say, "See if you can reach it to-day." Those who did not solve the first situation at the end of the fifth exposure were dropped from the Series. Since the solutions of the situations subsequent to Situation A of each Series are in a greater or less degree dependent upon the principle derived from Situation A in the respective Series, it was deemed best to eliminate those subjects who did not solve the key-situation of each Series so as to keep a homogeneous group made up of only those who had found the principle through the solving process, spontaneously—that is, without being taught. The exposures were limited to five, in consideration of the factor of interest which was found to be seriously on the wane at about that time and without which an exposure was a mere waste of time, as explained above.

For the second Series all the subjects were again started and eliminated in the same way as in Series I.

The instructions for this Series were somewhat different in nature. The subject was invited into the play-pen with "Come into this little house and see if you can get the little dog (or bird, airplane, etc.) out there." For subsequent exposures it was only necessary to say, "See, if you can get it to-day."

The second Series was not started until all children had been tried out on the first Series (with few exceptions in the case of absentees and late registrants). This kept the influence of the school situation upon the subject more nearly constant with respect to time, than if each subject had been run through both Series consecutively. It also provided a respite for the subject and avoided a flagging of interest in the experimenter and her games. Unlike similar experiments on animals where the motivating power is the satisfying of a biologic need—hunger—the experimenter's sole stock-in-trade when children are used as subjects, the *sine qua non* of the experiments, is interest. Hence, it is carefully guarded and deferred to.

So far as possible the experimenter sought to keep the intervals between exposures constant for all subjects, but this was seriously interfered with by absences. Constancy of intervals, however, appeared to the experimenter to be of minor importance, for variations did not seem to affect the subject's approach to the problem-situation.

EXPERIMENTER'S ATTITUDE

The experimenter established friendly relations with the subjects, even before the investigation was undertaken, by frequent visits to the Nursery School. This was reinforced with each individual child en route to the room in which the experiment was conducted. Once in the room and the instructions given, the experimenter sought to obliterate herself as nearly as possible. The subjects' chatter was unheeded. Persistent complaints and questions were answered briefly and in a matter-of-fact manner. But at the end of each exposure the subject who had failed to solve the problem was encouraged to hope for success on the following day and the one who had succeeded was duly congratulated.

GENERAL CHARACTER OF THE INVESTIGATION

In this series of experiments the writer strove to present situations to the subjects which would not be serious departures from their daily life at the Nursery School or at home; which would be so stimulating as to challenge them to action without undue urging on the part of the experimenter; and which would present problems difficult and varied enough to elicit a solving process representative of children at this age level.

It is hoped that the description of the nine test-situations shows beyond a doubt that the first aim was achieved; and that the activity of the subjects in these situations, to be described in a later chapter, answers fully for the second aim. Furthermore, the fact that a large number of the subjects at each age level were unable to solve some or all of the problems after repeated and varied effort indicates that they had actually run the gamut of resourcefulness and ingenuity on these problems.

The "games" were well liked and welcomed by the subjects, with the exception of a few of the youngest and most timid ones. A solution would yield the most extravagant joy and even ecstasy, not unlike the creative thrill experienced by adults under similar circumstances. Just as Köhler's genius-ape, Sultan, repeated the activity in the stick-joining experiment,[3] so, too, the human subjects would often repeat experiments as if for the joy of once more trying out a newly discovered and, what is more important, a self-discovered solution.

The experimenter tried to carry out Köhler's suggestion that the elements of the test-situation should be so placed as to be within sight of the subjects.[4] This was not always feasible after the first few moments of the exposure, for the subject would as

[3] Köhler, W., *The Mentality of Apes*, p. 133.
[4] *Ibid.*, p. 11.

likely as not turn his back on the block or the stick while reaching for the objective. Furthermore, the child is inclined to see things only on his own eye-level, with the result that the block or stick on the floor was often as invisible as though it were hidden.

THE RECORD

The experimenter kept a running account of each subject's activity in a test-situation; his remarks were taken down verbatim whenever they threw any light on the solving process, the total time spent at each exposure as well as the distribution of time over various activities was kept by means of a stop watch, the number of exposures required by each subject for the solution of each problem was noted, and the subject's age was recorded. These items constituted the complete record for each subject.

In the following chapter representative samples of these records will be presented and in subsequent chapters they will be referred to as illustrative material.

CHAPTER II

A PRELIMINARY SURVEY OF MATERIAL

TYPICAL CASES

Just as a statistical investigation is ideally represented in quantitative symbols, so an analytic, qualitative investigation such as this is would be ideally represented only by a moving picture of the subjects' activity. In the absence of this and as the only feasible substitute, partial records are submitted of twenty-two cases chosen with the view of illustrating all the different types of approach to a problem-situation exhibited by these subjects. In order that the reader may have a complete picture of a subject's solving behavior throughout the two Series, two cases will be recorded fully, that is, for all the exposures of the nine situations. Tables I-A and II-A give the same picture in symbolic form for all subjects.

In addition to the case material given in this chapter, other cases will be cited from time to time as illustrative of some specific findings to facilitate frequent reference to the case records.

Case 1

Subject: Boy, 40 months, II-C,[1] 17' 45".[2]

First exposure (4' 15") [3]—Subject grasped the short stick inside the pen, looked at the objective and indicated by his glance that he saw that the stick was too short; tried to reach with it the long stick outside. His movements were very jerky and impatient. Subject tried to reach long stick with his hand before it was close enough to the bars; tried to climb out of the pen, leaned over the top, shouting, "Stick." (1' 30") Subject looked about quietly; (2') reached for the long stick with his hand and appealed to Experimenter. He was distressed and angry

[1] This stands for the situation recorded—Situation C of Series II.
[2] This represents the total time spent by the subject in a given situation.
[3] This represents the time spent at one exposure.

and tried to force his way out of the pen. When Experimenter shook her head disapprovingly, Subject shouted, "Yes!"; began reaching for objective with his hand. Subject was on the verge of tears, so Experimenter ended the exposure, assuring him that he would have another chance. Once outside the pen, Subject grabbed the long stick, placed it close to the bars and begged Experimenter to leave it there!

Case 2

Subject: Girl, 38 months, I-A, 1'-.

First exposure (1')—Subject tried to reach balloon-objective with both hands but in 15 seconds looked around and said, "On box"; on her way to the block and as she carried it toward objective, complained, "I can't get it; you get it; it's too high." Subject placed block in good alignment, got on, and reached the objective with great joy.

Same Case, I-B, 25".

First exposure (25")—Subject ran eagerly toward airplane but swerved off to chair which she placed underneath objective, got on and reached, refusing to quit.

Same Case, I-C, 25".

First exposure (25")—Subject saw doll-objective on the shelf and cried, "Get it for me; I can't reach it." In 15 seconds she went for the block, placed it, and reached.

Same Case, I-D, 5'-.

First exposure (3')—Subject looked at objective and in 10 seconds went for the block, placed it, got on, tried to reach objective, and whined, "I can't reach it"; continued to complain; (2') ran over to a large, discarded flower-jug which was standing in a remote corner of the room and tried to drag it over to objective, saying, "Get it on this." Experimenter discouraged this on account of the weight of the jug; Subject refused to make further attempts to reach objective.

Second exposure (2')—At sight of objective, Subject shouted "Bird!"; looked at objective and asked whether other children had reached it; tried once to reach it by stretching up and (1' 30") said, "Can't get it." (1' 45") Subject went for block, which she placed on its perpendicular side, got on, and reached.

Same Case, 1-E, 7′ 30″–.

First exposure (4′)—Subject ran directly to grocery box, which she placed under objective and tried to reach up; complained and went off for block, placed it under objective, trying to reach it; jumped off almost at once and begged Experimenter to get it; (2′) seized grocery box and piled it on top of block, succeeding only in engulfing the latter. Subject appeared amused and startled, got on this pseudo-structure but jumped off without trying to reach. Disgusted and angry. Subject pulled the boxes apart and walked off. (3′ 15″) Subject piled block on top of grocery box but now the structure stood about 4 feet away from objective. Subject got on, her back to objective, and jumped off again, repeating this several times with great pleasure.

Second exposure, (3′ 30″)—Subject exclaimed at bird-objective, looked around and said, "You get big box; I can't get it"; (1′) went for grocery box, placed it on highest side, got on, and tried to reach objective; jumped off and said, "I can't get it"; (2′) went over to block, picked it up, and piled it on grocery box, got on, and reached objective.

Same Case, 40 months, II-A, 5′ 45″–.

First exposure (4′)—Subject handled the stick and talked about it before instructions were completed and then dropped it, trying to climb out of the pen to get objective; tried to reach objective by leaning over the top of pen, by stretching for it between the bars; sought an exit, repeating over and over, "I can't get birdie"; asked Experimenter to move objective closer; (2′) stepped on stick, looked down at it, and began to walk around. (2′ 30″) Subject picked up stick, banged with it on the wall, and threw it down; looked around and again tried to reach objective as before and by pushing her legs out between the bars. Subject appeared tired, and exposure was terminated.

Second exposure (1′ 45″)—Subject stretched for objective through the spaces, first with right hand and then with left, shouting, "To-day, I can get him"; tried to climb out and again reached through the spaces. (1′ 25″) Subject stepped on stick, pounced down on it, and used it for obtaining objective, which she had inside the pen by 1′ 35″; repeated the performance for fun.

Same Case, II-B, 20″–.

First exposure (20″)—Subject picked up broom at once and swept objective in deftly.

Same Case, II-C, 3′ 25″–.

First exposure (3′ 25″)—Subject tried to reach objective with the short stick and in 15 seconds threw it out. When Experimenter restored stick, Subject said, "Give me the other one, it's better." (1′) Subject threw stick out again and tried to climb out. Experimenter restored stick when Subject was not looking. (1′ 30″) Subject walked around and (1′ 45″) tried to reach objective again as before. (2′ 45″) Subject reached for long stick with the short one and then reached for objective with the long stick.

Same Case, II-D, 13′ 35″–.

First exposure (3′ 20″)—Subject examined one of the sticks and tried to reach objective with it over the top of pen; examined the other stick and used it in same way, repeating, "I can't" over and over; (1′) tried out the stick between the bars, over the top of pen, finally striking it viciously against the floor; complained bitterly and tried again to reach as before, stretching and straining; (2′ 45″) tried to climb out and whined, "I can't." Experimenter terminated exposure to avoid fatigue.

Second exposure (3′ 15″)—Subject reached for objective as above and in 10 seconds said, "Look, I can't," but continued her efforts; (45″) fitted sticks up against bars of pen, banged them together, etc. (2′) Subject tried to reach objective with her hand through the spaces, to force her way out, to shake the pen, etc.; (3′) said, "Dolly does not want me to get him."

Third exposure (3′)—As above, complaining intermittently and finally giving up.

Fourth exposure (4′)—Subject stretched for objective over the top of pen, striking out angrily with stick, complaining, and asking Experimenter to move objective closer. (1′ 45″) Subject said, "Let's try big stick on little one," picked up the other stick, examined ends carefully and succeeded in fitting them, with a shout of "Bang!" (1′ 50″) Subject angled for objective, reached it exultantly, and repeated stunt several times.

Case 5

Subject: Boy, 34 months, I-A, 29′–.

First exposure (5′)—Subject looked at the suspended duck for a few seconds and then at block for a long time and asked, "Who hanged it on the light?" Subject continued to look at block and objective and to fidget toward both; (3′ 15″) approached tentatively toward objective, with his right hand partly outstretched; but he withdrew his hand before having quite reached the objective; performed the rudimentary gesture of swinging objective, edging closer and closer toward it but finishing up by sticking his hands into his pockets and staring.

Second exposure (6′)—Subject appeared much interested in the suspended airplane; examined it from every angle, at a distance of 12 feet, asking many questions as, "Who put it on the light? How does it go?" His eyes traveled in the direction of the block several times. (5′) Subject slowly approached objective, with many glances at block en route. (All his movements were tentative as though he were not quite willing to commit himself.)

Third exposure (6′)—Subject greeted the objective with "Whose dolly is that? You swing it." (40″) Subject looked all around and said, "You swing the dolly. And the arms are not broken! I want dolly on the floor. She's tied to the light. I'll break her off if I pull." Experimenter assured him it was all right for him to swing the objective but Subject refused to try; (4′ 15″) went to the block, bent over it, examined it closely, shoved it a bit with his foot, and returned to the objective.

Fourth exposure (5′)—Subject looked at objective and asked, "What color is the duck? You swing it. How does John swing it?" (3′ 15″) Subject walked away to the opposite wall from where he continued to gaze at the objective.

Fifth exposure (5′)—On seeing the suspended balloon, Subject said, "I must take my coat off." He did so and then advanced slowly toward objective, passing it on his way to the opposite wall, from where he surveyed the objective. Experimenter asked him to swing objective, whereupon Subject made a rudimentary swinging gesture and looked with apparent misgivings at objective.

Same Case, 36 months, II-A, 7′ 15″–.

First exposure (7′ 15″)—When inside the pen, Subject asked, "Can I get through here?" indicating a space between the bars, just barely put his hand through and then his foot; looked around, discussing various details of the room; (1′ 15″) picked up the stick, put it through the space, and left it there, continuing to ask questions about the room, the pen, etc.; tried to squeeze through between the bars, sought an exit. (2′ 30″) Subject tentatively placed stick close to objective, shoving the latter a little farther away; became absorbed in inserting stick in spaces. Experimenter said, "We'll try to get the doll some other time," preparatory to closing the exposure, and Subject replied, "You get it now." Experimenter said, "The children play the game by getting the doll themselves," at which Subject very slowly began to angle for objective with the stick (6′ 15″) and had it inside the pen by 7′ 15″.

Same Case, II-B, 3′ 20″-.

First exposure, (3′ 20″)—Subject looked at objective, turned around and saw broom but returned to objective, reaching for it with his hand through the space. (1′) Subject turned upon the broom again, picked it up, and reached objective with it; repeated experiment as a game.

Case 9

Subject: Girl, 37 months, I-A, 28′-.

Second exposure (7′)—Subject was impressed with the balloon-objective and tried to reach it with her left hand; (15″) sat down opposite objective, occasionally looking at it. Experimenter swung objective and Subject ran to try her luck; reached for it first with right hand, then with left, and ran off; came back to reach up with both hands and ran off; walked around the room and again tried to reach objective, walked away and into the block; sat down on it but soon got up, lifted the block and moved it close to the wall; stood up on it and reached up to a shelf above, her back toward objective; began to walk around, paying no further attention to objective.

Third exposure (5′)—Subject looked at objective and then showed Experimenter an injured finger; ran around the room, came across the block, sat down on it, back to objective; got up and ran around again; (2′ 35″) came forward, arm outstretched toward objective, and then ran off.

Fourth exposure (4′)—Subject smiled at objective, turned to the block, looked at Experimenter and ran off; stood opposite objective, looking at it; (1′ 5″) approached the block tentatively and then walked off; (3′) ran up eagerly toward objective but made no attempt to reach it.

Fifth exposure (4′)—Subject looked wistfully at the suspended duck and was much pleased when Experimenter swung it; (1′) walked around, passing by the block; (2′) returned to the block, shoved it over to the wall and sat down on it, back toward objective, and there remained for one and a half minutes.

Case 10

Subject: Boy, 36 months, II-A, 4′–.

First exposure (4′)—When inside the pen, Subject sought an exit, tried to climb out and said, "I can't get out." (35″) Subject looked around, leaned over for the objective, and reached for it with right hand, complaining; stuck leg through space and complained that he could not get out that way, shouting, "Open the gate!"; tried to force his way out. (3′ 30″) Subject looked around, saw the stick and pounced on it, saying, "Let me have the stick to get the bird." Subject reached the objective very skilfully.

Same Case, II-B, 15″–.

First exposure (15″)—Subject cast one look at objective and swerved off for broom which he used to reach objective at once, repeating the experiment for fun.

Same Case, II-C, 6′–.

First exposure (5′)—Subject picked up the little stick and said, "I want the other stick, not the little one," and laid it down, demanding the long one from Experimenter; leaned over the top of the pen, sought an exit and whined, "It's too far away"; (1′ 50″) picked up the short stick, tried once to reach objective with it, and again began to whine, "I can't get it. You give me the big stick"; looked around, repeating his complaints and then concentrated on objective again, trying to reach it by sticking his leg out, leaning over and trying to climb out. Subject's complaints became too persistent, and the exposure was terminated.

Second exposure (1′)—On the way to the room, Subject said, "I'm going to get the big stick." When inside the pen, Subject picked up short stick, at once reached long stick with it, and then reached the objective with the long stick.

Case 11

Subject: Girl, 32 months, I-D, 40″–.

First exposure (40″)—Subject was fascinated by suspended

doll and ran at once for the block, which she placed on the lowest side, got on, and tried to reach objective; got off, turned block on its perpendicular side, got on, and reached the doll.

Case 13

Subject: Girl, 49 months, II-A, 15′ 30″–.

First exposure (3′ 30″)—Subject looked at the objective which she tried to reach over the top of pen, saying, "Look how short my hand is. I'll have to climb over"; looked around and tried to reach objective over the top by giving herself a head start. (1′ 15″) Subject pointed to the stick with her foot, saying, "What's that for? Shall I pick it up?" and after a pause, "Pretty little house"; shook the bars and jumped in place. "If you put it a little nearer I could get it." Subject made no other attempt to reach objective.

Second exposure (4′)—Before going into the pen Subject showed Experimenter where to put objective. When inside the pen she tried to climb out; (40″) walked around, protesting that her arm was too short; tried to reach objective by sticking her leg out and by reaching for objective over the top of pen; began to walk around, passed by the stick but appeared absorbed in other things; hummed and made no attempt to reach, nor did she show any interest in the situation.

Third exposure (3′)—Subject stretched to the utmost over top of the pen, saying, "I'll catch him in a minute"; turned away, picked up the stick and placed it on the molding extension; (1′ 30″) tried to reach objective as before; looked around and said, "That's a nice little house"; sat down on the stick and surveyed the field of action, saying, "Well, I can't catch him," and made no further attempt to reach objective.

Fourth exposure (2′)—Subject leaned over the top, stretching for objective desperately, giving herself a head start with each fling of the arm. (30″) Subject asked, "When are you going to have a different game?" (1′ 5″) Subject picked up the stick and placed it on the molding extension; began to walk around with elaborate indifference and swagger.

Fifth exposure (3′)—Subject leaned over the top of pen to reach objective and in 15 seconds, seeing the stick out of the corner of her eye, turned sharply around, picked up the stick and placed it on the molding extension with scrupulous precision;

(45″) returned to the objective and continued reaching for it as before. (1′ 15″) Subject said, "Maybe to-morrow I can reach it," and tried to get out of the pen. Subject appealed to Experimenter with "Let me give the doll to you," and threw many kisses at it.

Case 15

Subject: Boy, 39 months, I-A, 30″–.

First exposure (30″)—Subject was much distressed when asked to come with Experimenter, but at sight of the balloon-objective, he rushed at it trying to reach it with both hands. (10″) Subject turned round to complain to Experimenter, spied the block and announced tearfully that he would get on it; dragged block under objective, got on and reached up for it but found it rather a hard stretch; jumped off, turned block on its perpendicular side, got on and swung objective with great glee.

Same Case, I-B, 15″–.

First exposure (15″)—Subject looked at objective and ran off for chair, which he placed underneath objective, got on and swung objective.

Case 16

Subject: Girl, 44 months, I-A, 24′–.

First exposure (6′ 30″)—Subject approached suspended beads slowly with a showy indifference, saying, "I just like to walk for nothing"; walked around, looking occasionally at objective and at block, eyes traveling from one to the other once or twice. (3′) Experimenter asked Subject to swing objective, whereupon Subject approached to within two feet of objective, reached up to it with right arm, saying, "Up there," and walked off with, "I like to walk just for nothing"; returned to objective and tried to reach it, saying, "I can almost reach it"; looked up at objective and said, "I can't reach it"; began to walk around again, talking of her daily activities, casting many glances at objective and at block.

Second exposure (5′)—Subject approached the suspended doll but did not try to reach it; said, "You think my arm is as big as . . . " [Experimenter did not catch the full statement]; Subject walked away and (45″) tried to reach objective with left hand; withdrew it quickly, casting a self-conscious look at

Experimenter and said, "I am so tired, I can't reach anything to-day"; began to walk around with elaborate indifference, looking many times at objective.

[This subject displayed the same behavior throughout the five exposures, always making one or two attempts to reach and always rationalizing about her inability to do so, waxing more and more voluble with each failure.]

Case 17

Subject: Girl, 31 months, I-A, 28'–.

First exposure (5')—Looked at objective for 10 seconds, then all around; eyes traveled over the block and returned to it. Throughout the exposure, Subject remained in the same spot, apparently fascinated by airplane but making no attempt to reach it, even at the repeated suggestion of Experimenter.

Second exposure (6')—Subject rushed to objective and stretched up for it, first with right hand then with both, fairly vibrating because of the tension of her muscles; turned from time to time to look at Experimenter, alternating the use of her hands. (2' 10") Subject brought her arms down for the first time but her eyes were still riveted on objective; (3') reached for objective as before; (3' 20") walked a few steps away from objective and began to fuss with her clothes, looking at objective from time to time. Her eyes passed over the block again.

Third exposure (5')—Subject ran eagerly toward objective, slowed up and surveyed it from all sides; (30") reached up for objective with right hand, turning to look at Experimenter. Subject saw the block and took a few steps toward it, looked at Experimenter, stopped short, and began to examine her clothes. Subject continued to look with interest at objective but could not be induced to reach for it again.

[The remaining two exposures showed no variation in Subject's solving behavior, merely less absorption in the objective.]

Case 18

Subject: Girl, 42 months, I-A, 2' 30"–.

First exposure (2' 30")—Subject tried to reach suspended airplane with the right hand and with the left, then with both, shouting all the while, "It's too high; I can't do it. How do you get it?" She came to Experimenter with an outcry and was told to try again; reached up as before, complaining hurriedly and excitedly. (2′) Subject saw block, pounced on it and said with a sob, "I think this will help"; placed block in poor alignment but succeeded in swinging objective; radiant with joy. Subject jumped off, picked up block, tried to strike objective with it but failed and so placed block in better alignment, got on and swung objective once more, quitting reluctantly.

Same Case, 45 months, II-A, 17′ 40″–.

First exposure (2′ 15″)—Subject tried at once to get out as she came in and then by climbing over the top of pen and by squeezing through spaces. In despair, she asked, "How can we get out?" Subject lay down and tried to reach objective by stretching for it through spaces and began to cry at failure. Exposure was terminated with the assurance that Subject could reach objective some other time.

Second exposure (4′ 10″)—Subject reached through space for objective, staring at it as though in a trance; (35″) "I can't get dolly"; (1′) tried to reach objective as before and said, "What shall we do if we can't get it?"; tried the same method again, complaining, "I can't. It's too far. I can reach with my little hand only that far." [Subject was so distressed at her failure that she never left the bars nor looked around.]

Third exposure (4′)—Subject reached for objective as above and in one second began to walk around, saw the stick but continued to walk around. (2′ 45″) Subject tried once more to reach objective and burst out, "You put them too far away; that's why I can't get them!"; continued to stretch for objective.

Fourth exposure (3′ 45″)—Subject resorted to the same methods of reaching, complaining from time to time; (1′ 30″) began to walk around and in the course of her walk, stepped on stick but showed no recognition of the fact; (2′ 30″) tripped over the stick, looked down at it, and then returned to objective, reaching for it as before.

Fifth exposure (3′ 30″)—As above.

Case 19

Subject: Girl, 19 months, I-A, 20′–.

First exposure (3′)—Subject watched swinging duck with profound absorption and then began to look around, finger in mouth, remaining in the same spot throughout the exposure.

Second exposure (4′)—Subject was a little distressed but her attention was soon arrested by the swinging airplane. Experimenter asked Subject to swing objective whereupon Subject dropped the coat with which she had previously refused to part, advanced two steps toward objective and then retreated to her original position, from which she continued to look at objective from time to time.

Third exposure (3′)—Subject looked at suspended doll from a distance. At Experimenter's suggestion that she swing it, she came closer, seemed absorbed in the objective, but made no attempt to reach it.

Fourth exposure (5′)—Subject approached suspended duck with evident interest but stopped within about 8 feet of objective, looking at it; approached a few steps closer after a minute and then fastened her gaze upon Experimenter. (2′) Experimenter led Subject up to objective and swung it; Subject showed intense interest but did not move; began to play at peek-a-boo.

Fifth exposure (5′)—Subject walked right up to suspended doll, looked at it, at Experimenter, at block, at objective, and at Experimenter again, remaining in the same spot throughout; looked at the block again.

Case 20

Subject: Girl, 42 months, I-A, 21′ 20″–.

First exposure (4′)—Subject went up to objective, stared at it, and waveringly raised her left arm half way up, looking at Experimenter; remained thus for 2 minutes, then indicated that she wished her coat taken off. While adjusting her sweater sleeves, Subject caught sight of block, looked long and hard at it, then again partly outstretched her arm toward objective, looking at Experimenter; began to chew her nails, still staring at Experimenter.

Second exposure (4′)—Subject walked slowly up to objective and tried to reach it with her right hand, looking at Experimenter. Subject remained thus, with arm partly outstretched, gazing around, for 2 minutes. (2′ 15″) Subject looked at the block and took a few steps toward it, looking at Experimenter; alternated between a step toward block and attempt to reach up for objective; (3′) walked off, past the block, looking back at objective several times.

Third exposure (5′)—Subject looked at objective and at Experimenter, advanced slowly toward former, arm outstretched, reaching for objective in an ineffectual manner as she gazed all around; saw block but continued to reach up. (4′) Subject began to amuse herself with the woodwork on the nearest wall.

[The remaining two exposures showed no variation in Subject's solving behavior.]

Case 21

Subject: Boy, 42 months, I-A, 19′–.

First exposure (6′)—Subject reached up for suspended beads, first with one hand, then the other, and with both, stretching up on tiptoes and repeating over and over, "I can't reach up there." (1′ 30″) Subject turned to the shelf about five feet to the left of objective and was about to climb up on it but turned to ask Experimenter, "Do you mean up there?" pointing to objective. Experimenter nodded and Subject gave up attempt to climb [apparently because he perceived the gap between shelf and objective to be too great], but tried to reach objective as before, complaining all the while. Subject looked at block many times but was so absorbed in his failure as not to see it at all.

Second exposure (2′)—Subject tried to reach objective with both hands, repeating, "I can't reach it"; came to Experimenter, repeating this chant, almost with a sob. Receiving no assistance, Subject began to cry, and exposure was terminated with the promise that Subject would have another opportunity to reach objective.

Third exposure (5′)—Subject tried to reach objective as above, complaining and begging Experimenter to lift him up or to take down the toy, and finally said, "Don't take me here again because I can't reach it."

Fourth exposure (3′)—On the way to the testing room, Subject asked whether the objective would be low enough for him to reach. Once in the room, he tried to reach objective as above and in 15 seconds came to tell Experimenter that it was not low enough yet and that he would come back to try again some other time.

Fifth exposure (3′)—Subject tried to reach in the same way and in 15 seconds came to Experimenter to complain; asked to go back to the playroom, clung to Experimenter and disregarded objective. (2′) Sitting on a shelf near Experimenter, in full view of the complete field, talking to her of irrelevant matters, Subject suddenly said, "I'll try again," and looked for permission. Experimenter nodded approval and Subject jumped from his perch, ran to the block, placed it, and reached duck with chuckles.

Case 22

Subject: Boy, 42 months, II-A, 13′ 30″–.

First exposure (3′)—Subject began with, "I can't," then stuck right arm through space, reaching for objective and said, "It's too far"; tried again and again in the same manner, repeating after each attempt, "I can't do it." Subject looked only at objective and at Experimenter.

Second exposure (2′ 30″)—Subject again began with, "Can't get it," and tried to reach objective with his hand between bars. Throughout the exposure the same performance was repeated, interspersed with "I can't" and "I did try."

[The remaining three exposures were exact repetitions of this stereotyped behavior. Subject worked in a dogged, mechanical manner to the accompaniment of the above complaints uttered in a monotone.]

Case 26

Subject: Girl, 26 months, II-A, 20′–.

First exposure (4′ 15″)—Subject looked at duck-objective outside the pen and in 15 seconds tried to get her leg between bars; tried to reach objective by leaning over the top of pen, by climbing over, shaking the bars, searching for an exit and finally looking about. (1′ 25″) Subject said, "Show me how to get duck in here"; (1′ 45″) reached through the space for objective, first with one hand and then with the other; (2′ 15″) looked in the direction of stick and tried again to reach as before and looked around in a bewildered way.

Second exposure (4′ 30″)—Subject looked at objective for 10 seconds and then tried to reach as above; (1′ 5″) looked around, kicked stick back to the wall and tried to reach again; asked Experimenter if she could go upstairs.

Third exposure (4′)—Subject looked at objective for 15 seconds and then leaned over for it; (35″) looked around and shoved stick with her foot to the wall, then tried again to reach objective; (1′ 30″) tried to get out of pen, and finally asked to get out.

Fourth exposure (3′ 45″)—Subject looked at objective for 15 seconds and then tried to get out. (30″) Subject walked off, stepped on stick, picked it up and placed it on molding extension; (1′ 20″) returned to bars, trying to reach as before; (2′) tried to get out and (2′ 30″) said, "I want to get out," and made no further attempt to reach objective.

Fifth exposure (3′ 45″)—Subject looked at objective and in 10 seconds turned away and came across the stick; leaned over it as though to pick it up but checked herself and looked at Experimenter; (25″) placed stick on molding extension and then tried to reach objective as above; (1′ 45″) "I want to get out." Experimenter urged her to try again, whereupon she repeated above performance.

Case 28

Subject: Boy, 39 months, I-C, 15″–.

First exposure (15″)—Subject caught sight of objective on the shelf at once, went directly for the block, placed it with an eye on the objective, got on and reached it.

Case 30

Subject: Boy, 49 months, II-A, 3′ 15″–.

First exposure (3′ 15″)—Subject looked at objective over top of the pen and in 5 seconds began to look around; sat down and peered through the bars; (25″) "I'll go out and get the dog in," to which Experimenter replied by shaking her head negatively. (40″) Subject picked up stick, looked at Experimenter, and very tentatively put the stick through the space, again looked at Experimenter and drew stick in before it was half way out; placed it where he originally found it. (1′ 45″) Subject tried to reach objective with left hand through space, saying, "It's too far," but continued to stretch for it; (2′ 30″) tried to reach with stick again, succeeded and was thrilled when the toy was in his hand.

Same Case, II-D, 5′ 15″–.

First exposure (3′)—Subject examined sticks and tried to reach objective with one of them, pushing it through space.

(25″) "I can't reach it with this stick. I must have another big stick." With the help of one stick, Subject shoved the other out as far as it would go toward objective. He appeared disconcerted at the loss of the stick, and Experimenter restored it; (1′ 30″) stuck finger into the hole at one end of the stick and then tried to fit both sticks together. Finding this difficult, Subject tried to fit them at two other ends and succeeded in inserting one end into the other but the result was a loose, wobbly affair. With this unstable structure, Subject attempted to angle for objective by holding on with his hand at the place of juncture. The sticks fell apart and Subject said, "Ah, I can't get the duck. To-morrow you'll have stick that holds."

Second exposure (2′ 15″)—Subject tried to reach objective by putting both sticks outside the bars and said, "He's too far"; turned his back on the objective and played with the sticks against the wall; returned to objective, tried to reach with one stick, then examined both, fitted them carefully and reached for objective successfully.

Case 39

Subject: Boy, 27 months, II-A, 5′–.
First exposure (5′)—Subject walked around, sought an exit, stepped on the stick, looked at it and then tried to force his way out, distressed, moaning and beating at the bars like a caged animal; tried to climb out. (2′ 20″) Subject looked at stick, picked it up and said, "What's this?"; played around with it and (3′) began to beat the duck with it, clumsily throwing it one way and another, enjoying himself tremendously. When objective was near the bars, Subject took it in.

Same Case, II-B, 2′ 15″–.
First exposure (2′ 15″)—Subject stuck his leg out through the space and whined for objective; (15″) walked over to the broom but turned his back on it; sought an exit; reached for objective over top of the pen; tried to squeeze through space, and moaned. (1′ 30″) Subject picked up broom and used it skilfully for objective, saying, "See."

Case 42

Subject: Boy, 32 months, I-A, 12′ 30″–.
First exposure (3′)—Subject looked up at suspended bird;

appeared shy and self-conscious, looking intently at his fingers, buttons, etc.; began to look around the room, always with an eye on objective, and then to walk around in small circles, never leaving objective for more than a few seconds. During one such round Subject walked into block (his back toward objective), stopped for a second and continued around the circle back to objective; came in contact with block once more in an unseeing way.

Second exposure (5′ 30″)—Subject ran over eagerly to suspended dog, looked at it and began to survey his hands; walked around objective, surveying it from every angle, and again examined his hands, showing Experimenter some scratches on his fingers; asked her to roll up his sleeves, interrupting the performance from time to time to go over to objective, talking to Experimenter rapidly about it. [During these declamations he stood directly in front of block but appeared to take no notice of it.] (4′ 45″) Subject saw block, bent down as if to take it, but checked himself; walked away and around, then returned to objective.

Third exposure (3′)—Subject tried many times to reach suspended duck with right hand, saying about fifty times, "Can't, can't, can't catch duck"; came to Experimenter with the same chant and then returned to objective, reaching for it as before and at the same time looking around the room; (2′) caught sight of block, pushed it over, asking, "Stand on block?" He carefully aligned block with objective, got on, and was ecstatically happy to reach the objective. Subject wanted to know why he couldn't take objective down, and turned block on its perpendicular side in an attempt to do so.

Same Case, I-B, 25″-.

First exposure (25″)—Subject ran toward objective but immediately swerved off to the chair; placed it under objective, got on, and reached.

Same Case, I-C, 35″-.

First exposure (35″)—Immediately upon entering the room, Subject shouted, "Can't reach the duck," and ran off for the block, which he placed on its perpendicular side, got on and reached with great glee.

Same Case, I-D, 4′-.

First exposure (4′)—Subject placed block underneath objective, got on, tried to reach it, and said, "I can't"; got off, lifted the block above his head, trying to strike objective with it, but it fell out of his hands, causing him to lose his balance and fall. He got up immediately, placed block on its perpendicular side, got on and reached objective. Subject was overjoyed and loath to leave the room.

Same Case, I-E, 13′ 30″–.

First exposure (3′ 30″)—Subject surveyed the field and went directly for the block, which he placed on its perpendicular side underneath objective, got on and said, "I can't"; (1′) went for grocery box, dragged it over to objective, got on and tried to reach objective, ending with, "I can't do it," after which he ran off. (2′ 15″) Subject got on box again, reached up for objective and in a disheartened voice, said, "I can't"; jumped off, began to put on his hat and gloves, ready to quit.

Second exposure (4′ 30″)—Subject was fascinated by the dog-objective and stared at it for 10 seconds, finally saying, "I can't get it up there. I can't reach it any more," and refused to try again. (45″) Subject tried to strike at objective with his hat but after two such attempts ran off to the other side of the room and refused to make another effort to reach objective.

Third exposure (5′ 30″)—Subject ran off for grocery box, which he placed on its perpendicular side, eyes on objective while doing so; tried to reach objective and jumped off; turned the box 100 degrees, still on its highest side, got on again, reached up for objective and jumped off; turned box on its lower side, got on, tried to reach objective, and complained of his failure. (1′ 45″) Subject ran away and began to play a little game of his own. When Experimenter urged him to try again, Subject emphatically told her he could not reach objective. (3′ 30″) Subject went for block again, placed it on its highest side, got on and tried to reach objective, announcing, "I can't reach it"; got off and walked away. (4′ 45″) Subject ran over to the block, placed it on top of grocery box, moved structure underneath objective, got on and reached it, overwhelmed with joy.

Same Case, 37 months, II-A, 3′ 45″–.

First exposure (3′ 45″)—Subject looked at objective outside the pen and in 10 seconds tried to reach it by sticking his arm through the spaces, first the right then the left, saying after each attempt, "I can't"; sought an exit, tried to climb out, stuck his leg through the space, tried again to reach with his hand, saying over and over, "See, I can't." (1' 45") Subject looked around in a distressed and unseeing way in the direction of the stick; (2') reached again as before, sought an exit, asked Experimenter to move objective closer; (3') looked in the direction of the stick, pounced on it, and carefully moved objective with it to where he could reach objective with his hand.

Same Case, II-B, 40"–.

First exposure (40")—Subject grasped broom at once and reached objective; repeated performance for fun.

Same Case, II-C, 4' 15"–.

First exposure (4' 15")—Subject tried to reach airplane with short stick and then tried to climb out; made one attempt to reach long stick and then, aiming at objective, threw the short stick out at it, not viciously, but merely to establish contact with objective, it would seem. Experimenter casually replaced the stick. (1') Subject pleaded, "May I have the other stick?" pointing excitedly at long stick; threw short stick out at long stick, and Experimenter once more returned it to the pen. (2' 15") Subject reached the long stick with short one and then reached objective with the former.

Same Case, II-D, 3'–.

First exposure (3')—Subject reached for objective with both sticks over the top of the pen and in 10 seconds said, "I can't reach it," repeating the complaint over and over; (25") reached for objective with one stick over the top, striking out viciously and finally throwing stick at objective; (1') reached for objective with his hand through space, stretching to the utmost and complaining; (1' 30") appealed to Experimenter; (1' 45") picked up the other stick, with which he drew in the first, examined them, tried fumblingly to fit one into the other. He interrupted his performance with frequent looks and jerks toward objective. Subject began to redden under the strain, and Experimenter helped to join the sticks by holding them at the middle so as to steady them.[4] Subject reached for objective at once.

[4] Experimenter took the liberty to assist here and in other cases where the solution was so obviously consummated in Subject's mind, as borne out by his gestures and his behavior in general. The difficulty in such cases is a purely motor one and, in fact, partly due to the eagerness to try out the solution which appears to be already clearly defined in Subject's mind. Where this was not so obvious, Experimenter did not render the service.

Case 43

Subject: Girl, 32 months, I-A, 2′–.

First exposure (2′)—Subject dashed at suspended duck, right hand outstretched, not giving Experimenter a chance to remove her hat and coat. When Subject found she could not reach objective, she began to rip her things off. That accomplished, she immediately picked up block, placed it directly under objective, and snatched at objective.

Same Case, II-A, 4′ 45″–.

First exposure (3′ 30″)—Subject reached with her hand over the top of the pen, shook the bars, stuck her leg out through the space, sought an exit, again shook the pen, tried to reach objective with her hand over the top of pen, leaning over as far as she could, repeating in rapid staccato, "I can't get it"; looked around, directly at stick, at objective outside the pen, at Experimenter. (2′ 30″) Subject reached as before and looked around bewildered.

Second exposure (1′ 15″)—Subject stuck her leg outside the bars, shook the bars, and in 15 seconds picked up the stick and said, "Stick"; waved it tentatively outside and then suddenly began to angle for objective as though the idea had just occurred to her.

Same Case, II-B, 25″–.

First exposure (25″)—Subject used the broom for objective at once and deftly.

Case 44

Subject: Girl, 32 months, II-A, 40″–.

First exposure (40″)—Subject looked around and in 5 seconds turned upon the stick, grasped it and clumsily worked it over top of pen until objective was close enough to reach with her hand.

CHAPTER III

ANALYSIS OF MATERIAL: THE RESPONSE

From the point of view of the subject, his activity in the problem-situations described in Chapter I should be considered as a continuous experience, beginning with the first sight of the objective and ending naturally with the solution of the problem or abruptly with the last exposure in the absence of a solution. From the point of view of the problem, however, the subject's activity may be divided into his first response to the problem-situation, which may and may not be synonymous with the solving process, and the solution itself. An analysis of the response is here undertaken.

The children's responses to problem-situations varied widely, as widely as their personalities. Yet it is by no means impossible to make some classifications. The first and most obvious classification that suggests itself is on the basis of the above implication that the response and the solving process are not necessarily synonymous. Thus we would have in one small group those subjects who made no or almost no attempt to solve. Their response was either weeping at being removed from the playroom or silent, sometimes sullen, watching of the objective. Case 19, cited in Chapter II, is illustrative. In the other group would fall all the other subjects who made a more or less consistent effort to get the objective. The other cases cited in the preceding chapter are illustrative. The frequency of each class is as follows:

1. No attempt to solve (Negative Response) 4 children, or 25 per cent.

2. Definite attempt to solve (Positive Response) 40 children, or 75 per cent.

The ages of the children in Class 1 are 19, 23, 27, and 28 months respectively. Though among the youngest, they were not actually the youngest, with the exception of Case 19 who was 19 months old. Chronological age is therefore hardly enough to explain this unresponsiveness.

The mental ages of these subjects (derived from Kuhlmann-Binet tests) are 20.4, 30, 31.5, and 33 months respectively. Again though among the lowest, they are not actually the lowest except Case 19, 20.4 months. Subjects with mental ages lower than the other three not only made definite attempts to reach the objective, but actually solved one or more problems. Besides, the correlation between mental ages and solutions is very low, only $+ 0.266$. Thus mental age, likewise, is not an adequate explanation of unresponsiveness. Nor can we satisfactorily explain unresponsiveness on the basis of interest for we would still be without an explanation of the absence of interest.

It appears more than likely that the failure of these four subjects to respond positively to the toy-reaching situation is due to immaturity, both social and emotional. Just as children of the same chronological age may vary in physical and mental development, so they may also vary in their social and emotional development. These four children were loath to leave the room to which they had become accustomed; they were apprehensive about entrusting themselves to the experimenter, and their attitude toward the situation in the examining room was highly colored by this displeasure, more or less actively expressed. It may therefore be said that these subjects were responding primarily, not to the test-situation but to the change in routine. This may fairly be called a socially and emotionally immature response.

Another classification suggests itself on the basis of directness of Response. Into the first class would fall those children whose first reaction is an overt, unmistakable attempt to reach the objective, as Case 43, I-A, page 27. For these subjects the situation is so compelling as to make instructions hardly necessary. Into the second class would fall those who do not so commit themselves to action, but rather stand off, observe the objective and talk about it or some irrelevant matter before attempting to reach for it, as Case 42, I-A, page 23, or Case 16, I-A, page 16. (It is of interest to note that Cases 42 and 43, representing antithetical behavior, are twins.) It can hardly be said that for these subjects (except the four mentioned above and included here) the situation as a situation is less compelling, but rather that they cannot so readily forget themselves. The frequency for these two classes is:

1. Direct response.............30 children, or 68 per cent.
2. Indirect response.............14 children, or 32 per cent.

This division suggests Jung's two classes, Extravert and Introvert, the former responding readily to his objective environment and the latter "interposing a subjective view between the perception of the object and his own action" [1] which serves inevitably to inhibit direct action. Such a classification is, however, better designed to throw light upon types of personality than upon types of response.

If we are now to consider the response as synonymous with the solving process, that is, as an actual attempt to reach the objective, we find that four distinct types stand out:

1. *The Primitive Response.*—This refers to the act of reaching for the objective with the hand. Such a reaction is inherent in the situation and is consequently often merely the forerunner of other responses. For example, it often happens that the child reaches up for the objective immediately upon entering the room, without having had time to see what else there is. After one or two such attempts, the child does look about, sees the block or stick, and uses it correctly at once. Or it may happen that the child who has already learned to use the stick or block will reach for the objective with his hand once or twice, as if in spite of himself, and then use the stick or block. Again, it may happen that a child who has already discarded the Primitive Response as a means of reaching the objective, will, when faced with a dilemma—an insoluble problem—revert to the Primitive Response. It is because of this prepotent nature of the response, overdetermined as it is by both the situation and the subject's customary reaction to such a situation, that it is here called the Primitive Response. The word as used here has no phylogenetic connotations, hardly any intended ontogenetic connotations, though the reaching reaction at the sight of an object does happen to be one of the earliest in the development of the child, occurring as it does about the sixteenth week. Cases 43, I-A; 42, I-A-3 [2]; 42, II-D; and 30, II-A are illustrative of the different varieties of this type of Response.

[1] Jung, C. G., *Psychological Types*, Harcourt, Brace & Co., 1926.
[2] The figure 3 refers to the exposure.

2. *The Random Response.*—Objectively this corresponds almost exactly to the reaction of Thorndike's cats when confined in the puzzle-box:

> When put into the box the cat would show evident signs of discomfort and of an impulse to escape from discomfort. It tries to squeeze through any opening; it claws and bites [3] at the bars and wires; it thrusts its paws out through any opening and claws at everything it reaches; it continues its efforts when it strikes anything loose and shaky.[4]

On the whole, the desire to escape confinement plays only a minor rôle with children in these situations, the major concern being to get the objective upon which attention is riveted throughout the experiment, as is plainly judged by the facial expression, by the repeated attempts to reach, and by what the subject says. One is therefore justified in saying that though the external picture of the subject in this situation often resembles that of the cat in the box, the underlying cause of such behavior is more resentment at being thwarted than distress at confinement and is in this respect comparable to the outburst of chimpanzees under similar circumstances.[5]

The emotional tone and tempo of activity is the characteristic feature of this response. The subject is either distressed as Case 18, I-A, page 17, or violent as Case 39, II-A, page 23. The solving process in any case is carried on jerkily and impetuously. The Random Response in children may occur at the outset of an experiment or after the subject has made other futile attempts to reach the objective.

3. *Exploration and Elimination.*—This refers to a deliberate trying out (again on the basis of emotional tone and tempo of activity) of one possibility after another or an investigation of the constituent parts of a situation. Sometimes this Response is guided by a partial understanding of or insight into the situation as with Case 5, II-A and Case 30, II-A, but more often it is of a lower order, guided only by the subject's desire for the objective out of reach, as with Case 5, II-D and Case 11, I-D.

4. *Immediate Solution.*—This Response is exhibited where no apparent problem seems to exist, as in Cases 28, I-C and 44, II-A. Ordinarily it occurs at the outset of the exposure, as its name

---

[3] This does not hold true for the subjects in the present study.
[4] Thorndike, E. L., "Animal Intelligence," p. 35. Macmillan, 1911.
[5] Köhler, *The Mentality of Apes*, p. 48. Harcourt, Brace & Co., 1925.

implies, but included in this class are also those solutions which are preceded for a brief interval by the Primitive Response, allowing for a period of orientation. Such an allowance is defensible in the light of what was said about the Primitive Response on page 30.

Table I-A gives a complete picture of each subject with reference to Types of Response throughout the two Series, while Tables I-B and I-C give the frequency of each response in the two Series.

Several facts are disclosed by these tables:

First, that the response fits the situation. Thus the Primitive Response is seen to become less and less frequent as the test-situations and the idea of "tools" become more and more familiar. Note the drop in frequency after the first situation of each Series. When it occurs at all in subsequent situations it is a temporary reversion to a prepotent response or gesture due to momentary forgetfulness or to a lapse in resourcefulness, as when the subject is face to face with a dilemma. Note also the infrequency of the Random Response in Series I as compared to Series II, where a semblance of confinement and a greater number of details are introduced into the test-situations. Only two subjects exhibit this response in Series I, and even in these cases the term is more descriptive of the emotional tone than of the method. As one might expect, the fall and the rise in frequency of the Exploration and Elimination Type of Response conform directly with the fall and the rise in the difficulty of the test-situations and inversely with the frequency of Immediate Solutions.

Second, that a subject does not consistently adhere to one Type of Response but varies it in accordance with the needs of the situation. This may be regarded as a corollary of the first observation.

Third, that Exploration and Elimination is the most frequent Type of Response, the Primitive Response is a close second, and the Random Response is relatively very infrequent.

This table throws additional light on the relation between problem-situations and solving procedure. In showing that the same child varies his response from more or less random manipulation to more or less deliberate experimentation in accordance with the set-up of the problem, it places emphasis on the problem

TABLE I-A
Types of Response in Individual Cases

Case	Sex	Age (Series I)	A	B	C	D	E	Age (Series II)	A	B	C	D
1	B	3-3	P E P	I	I	E P E	E	3-4	E I	I	E R E	E
2	G	3-2	P I	I	I	E P E	E P E	3-4	E P	I	E P E	E R
3	B	3-3	P	I	I	E	E	3-5	P	I	E	E
7	G	2-6	E P E	E	I	E P	E P	2-9	E	E P	E	E
10	B	2-9	P R P R	I	I	E	E	3-0	E R	I	E R	E P E
11	G	2-8	E P	P I	E I	E	E	2-10	R I	E I	E I	E
12	G	2-5	P E P	P I	P E P	E	E	2-7	E P E	I	E	E
14	B	4-1	P E P E	I	I	I	E	4-3	E	P E	P E	P E
15	B	3-3	P I	I		I	I	3-5	E	I	P E	E
21	B	3-6	P E P	P I	I	E	E	3-8	E	I		E
27	B	3-3	P E P	I	I	E	E	3-5	I	I	P E	E
28	B	3-2	P E	P I	I	E	E	3-4	P I	I	I	E
35	G	1-11	P E P	I	E P E	E P	E P	2-3	E	I	E P	E
41	B	2-11	P I	P I	I	I	E	3-4	E P E	P	I	E
42	B	2-8	P E	I	I	E	E	3-1	P E	I	E	E P E
43	G	2-8	P I	P I	P I	P E	P E	3-2	R	I	I	E
4	G	2-11	P E P	I	I	I	E	3-1	P E P			
5	B	2-10	E					3-0	E	P	E	E
6	G	3-2	P					3-5	E P E P			
8	G	2-4	E	P I	P I	P E	E P	2-7	E R P			
9	G	3-1	P					3-4	R E	I	E	E
13	G	3-10	P I	P I	I		E	4-1	E			
16	G	3-8	P					3-9	P E P			
17	G	2-7	P					2-10	E P			
18	G	3-8	P R	I	I	E	E	3-9	P E P E			
19	G	1-7	P						Used for	this	Series	
20	G	3-8	P					3-9	P E P E			
22	B	3-4	P E P					3-6	P E P			
23	G	3-4	E P					3-6	E	I	E	E
24	G	3-8	P E	P I	P I	E P E	P E P	3-9	E P			
25	G	2-4	E P					2-5	No Res	pon	se	
26	G	2-1	P					2-2	E P R P			
29	G	2-6	P E P					2-9	I	I	R E R	R E
30	B	3-10	P E P					4-1	E P	I	P	E
31	B	2-11	I	I	E	E P	E	3-3	E	Left	school	
32	G	2-3	No Res	pon	se				Not used	for	this Se	ries
33	G	2-8	P E	I	I	P	E P	3-0	E P			
34	G		Not used	for	this	Series		2-0	E	P	P E	E
36	B	1-11	P E					2-5	R P R E	R E	R E	E
37	G	1-11	P						Left sch	ool		
38	B		Not used	for	this	Series		2-6	R E R			
39	B		Not used	for	this	Series		2-3	R	P	E P E R	E R
40	G	2-10	P E P					3-4	E	I	I	E
44	G		Not used	for	this	Series		2-8	I	I	P E P	E P

NOTE: The letters P R E I stand for the four Types of Response described earlier in the chapter—Primitive, Random, Exploration and Elimination, Immediate Solution. Under each situation the letters appear in the order in which the Types of Response appeared. Thus P E P means that the subject started out with the Primitive Response, changed to Exploration and Elimination and back to the Primitive Response, in the same or successive exposures.

In cases where the record ends with the first situation, it is to be understood that the subject failed and was therefore dropped from the Series, unless other explanation is given.

TABLE I-B

Frequency of Types of Response

Response Type	Series I							Series II						Both Series	
	Test-Situation					Total	Per Cent	Test-Situation				Total	Per Cent	Total	Per Cent
	A	B	C	D	E			A	B	C	D				
P	48	9	6	9	8	80	38	26	6	10	4	46	24	126	32
R	3	0	0	0	0	3	.2	12	1	6	3	22	12	25	6
E	24	1	5	20	24	74	35	36	4	23	28	91	48	165	41
I	6	22	19	4	1	52	25	6	19	5	0	30	16	82	21
No. of Cases	40	23	22	22	23			41	26	25	26				

NOTE: The symbols used in this table represent the same terms as those used in Table I-A. The frequency for each Type of Response, as given in this table represents a simple addition of all the P's, R's, E's, and I's found in each test-situation in Table I-A. But since this table is meant to give a picture of each individual with reference to Types of Response, a Response may be repeated several times in the same situation, which explains the large totals in reference to the number of cases. In Table I-C the frequency of each Type of Response is derived from a single count of each type in each situation for each subject.

TABLE I-C

Response Type	Series I					Total	Series II				Total	Total of Both Series	Per Cent
	Test-Situation						Test-Situation						
	A	B	C	D	E		A	B	C	D			
P	36	9	5	9	7	66	19	6	9	4	38	104	30
R	2	0	0	0	0	2	10	1	5	3	19	21	6
E	22	1	4	18	21	56	32	4	20	27	83	139	40
I	6	22	19	4	1	52	6	19	5	0	30	82	24

NOTE: The symbols used in this table represent the same terms as those used in Table I-A.

rather than the subject. This is confirmed by the results of Ruger's [6] experiments with wire-puzzles which show that intelligent adults may respond in a manner formerly considered typical of animals, if faced with problems obscurely organized. In other words, whether the subject be an animal, a child, or an

[6] Ruger, H. A., *The Psychology of Efficiency.* Archives of Psychology, No. 15, June, 1910.

adult, different types of response may be provoked by changing the set-up of the problem.

Assuming, then, that there are different types of response, however named, what relation do these bear to the solution itself? The next chapter will undertake to answer this question.

CHAPTER IV

ANALYSIS OF MATERIAL: THE SOLUTION

The Response or activity preceding the solution can be interpreted in two ways: either it is instrumental in bringing about a fortuitous but none the less suggestive constellation of the elements of a problem-situation, which constellation is in effect the solution itself; or else it yields the subject an understanding of, or insight, into the problem-situation upon which the solution depends.

To determine which interpretation is correct, the reader is referred to the Case Records cited in Chapter II. These give only an imperfect picture of the subjects' activity, omitting, as it must, much of the change in facial expression and posture which only a moving picture camera could capture. If it is found that a solution was effected by a random manipulation of the block or stick which accidentally brought subject, block or stick, and objective into a suggestive relationship identical with the solution, insight must be rejected as an explanation of that solution. But if the subject used the stick or block as a means for the objective as the end, then it may be concluded that the subject saw the relatedness of parts, that is, stick or block, objective, and himself, constituting the whole—desired objective out of reach but attainable with the help of the stick or block. In other words, the solution is accompanied by insight.

Such decisions may be rendered even in the absence of reliable, objective criteria of insight for the reader is sufficiently familiar with chance solutions to identify them and may rely upon the process of elimination to select the others. But this is not the only way, for insight, fortunately, may also be readily identified. A hypothetical case will serve as an illustration:

An adult subject is trying to solve an unfamiliar wire puzzle, such as Ruger used for his subjects.[1] We see him making one tentative move after another, hopefully repeating formerly un-

[1] Ruger, H. A., *The Psychology of Efficiency.* Archives of Psychology, No. 15, June, 1910.

successful moves and presenting in general a picture of perplexity. Suddenly the subject may say, "Oh, I see," and in a few more seconds, the puzzle is solved. We do not hesitate to say that at a particular point in the solving process, just before the subject uttered the above exclamation, the material in hand underwent a definite change from a disorganized, meaningless mass to an organized, meaningful arrangement of parts, or often from an inappropriate to a more appropriate organization. Obviously this change is not in the material but in the subject, and when it occurs the subject may be said to have gained insight into the problem. The solution itself thus becomes the criterion of insight. In Köhler's words, " . . . a complete solution with reference to the whole lay-out of the field" [2] is the criterion of insight. Or as Koffka understands Köhler's statement, " . . . the manipulation of things with reference to their important material relations can be employed as a criterion of behavior with insight." [3]

The point at which the subject exclaims, "Oh, I see," may then be regarded as the turning point of the solving process. Whatever may be said of his manipulations prior to that exclamation, it is certain that subsequent to it, they are "with reference to the whole field" (barring, of course, the few exceptions where the subject is misled by a false cue). Nor is the "Oh, I see" an indispensable indicator of insight to the experimenter for the action pattern of the subject undergoes an unmistakable change at this point. His facial expression, his posture, the tempo at which he works, and the precision with which he works all reflect his newly acquired slant. Ruger's term *analysis* is partially synonymous with insight and his subjective description of it is particularly applicable to the experience of insight, "the experience of analysis is distinct from that of ordinary perception . . . and from that of a motor impulse. It is oftentimes a striking experience and seems to come with a rush or as a flash." [4] Miss Heidbreder found that for her adult subjects "a new mode of perceiving" was one of the outstanding features of their experience.[5] This "new mode of perceiving" is, like insight, the result of a subjective reorganization of the problem.

[2] Köhler, p. 198. *The Mentality of Apes.* Harcourt, Brace & Co., 1925.
[3] Koffka, K., *The Growth of the Mind*, p. 217. Harcourt, Brace & Co., 1925.
[4] Ruger, *Op. cit.*, p. 13.
[5] Heidbreder, Edna, *An Experimental Study of Thinking.* Archives of Psychology, **73, 1924.**

Since there is agreement among those who have directly or indirectly studied insight that it emerges in a more or less spectacular manner and is therefore easily recognized, cannot those features which characterized insight be used as criteria of insight, to be checked by the solution itself? Changes in the subject's facial expression and in posture, the tempo at which and the precision with which he works, and verbalization are such features; and we propose that they be used, in terms of the solution, as Primary Criteria of insight, to be supplemented and confirmed by Transfer and Retention as Secondary Criteria, to which reference will be made later.

According to the judgment of those who have watched the subjects at work and those who have read the running account of their activity, all trained psychologists, there seems to be no doubt whatever as to the presence of insight. In fact, the set-up of the problem-situations in such as almost to preclude any other solution, however likely to occur such solutions are in problems of the puzzle-box or wire-puzzle type which allow the factor of chance greater play.

If this whole question is regarded for the time being outside the setting of theoretical implications, the assumption that the solutions of the present problem-situations were accompanied by insight is not only warranted but inevitable and even obvious. What is not obvious is how insight evolved, and this appears to the writer to be the crux of the problem to which the remainder of this study is devoted, incidentally throwing some further light upon the fact of insight.

TYPES OF SOLUTION

The Immediate Solution which has already been considered as one Type of Response may now serve as an introduction to the question of Types of Solution. The Immediate Solution, we have seen, comes as a result of complete and immediate insight into the problem, that is, where no problem actually exists for the subject.

Where the solution is not immediate, insight is evolved in the course of the solving process in one of two ways: gradually, when it is preceded by the subject's betrayal of his awareness of the presence of the block or stick; or suddenly, when it occurs unpreceded by his betrayal. Such betrayals of awareness may be expressed by a long and hard look at the block or stick, by kicking it, by carrying it around, by changing its location, by shifting its position. As a matter of fact these contacts between the subject and the block or stick often indicate more than mere awareness of its presence. The subject seems to sense a cue; thus these contacts are, in many cases, glimmerings of insight. However, one is not obliged to commit oneself to this interpretation.

It is obvious, of course, that a subject may be aware of the presence of the block or stick without betraying it by his behavior, and when he finally uses the one or the other correctly and with insight, this insight seems to have emerged *suddenly,* unheralded by betrayals, without warning, as it were.

The reader's attention is directed to the fact that the word *sudden* has no reference to the "rush" with which insight usually comes to a head, whether gradual or sudden in its onset. This "rush" or "flash" or "jerk" quality (these are only a few of the terms used by writers to describe insight) is inherent in the nature of insight. (See quotations from Ruger and Heidbreder, page 37.)

To further clarify this distinction between solutions with *gradual* and with *sudden* insight, the reader is referred to Case 43, II-A, cited on page 27, which illustrates the former type and to Cases 21, I-A and 18, I-A, pages 20 and 17, as illustrative of the latter type. In Case 43, II-A, examples of betrayals of awareness are: "looked around directly at the stick, at objective outside the pen, and at Experimenter" . . . "picked up the stick and said, 'Stick'" . . . "waved it [stick] tentatively outside. . . . " It is clear that in Cases 18 and 21 there are no such betrayals.

Nothing has thus far been said about the degree of insight accompanying a solution. Yet the writer cannot assert with Koffka and Köhler that "an appropriate transformation of the field precedes the objective solution" [6] invariably. Though this is true of most solutions, there are cases of which it is more accurate to say that "an appropriate transformation of the field" occurs coincidentally with the solution, possibly continuing after the act of solution is completed. It may be said of these solu-

[6] Koffka, K., *The Growth of the Mind,* p. 205. Harcourt, Brace & Co., 1925.

tions that they are accompanied by *partial* insight, gradually evolved, as contrasted with solutions accompanied by *complete* insight, illustrated by Case 43, II-A, already referred to. Though insight is here evolved gradually during the process of Exploration and Elimination, there can be no doubt that when the subject begins to reach "as though the idea had just occurred to her," she does so with *complete* insight. An almost tangible break occurs when she ceases to wave the stick outside uncertainly and reaches for the objective with assurance. The ease with which the basic principle of Situation A is seen to be carried over to Situation B is further proof that complete insight was present when the solution occurred. The relation between transfer and insight previously referred to (page 38) will be discussed later.

For contrast let us now examine Case 39, II-A, page 23, which illustrates a solution with *partial* insight. Here again insight matured gradually, but, judged by the Primary Criteria of insight, given on page 38, it remained partial even after the solution. At the point where the subject began to beat the duck, there was no definite break in attitude. To the experimenter it appeared to be a continuation of his play with the stick but more exploratory and better defined. When the subject saw the duck at the bars his expression still showed wonder as much as enlightenment. If we now turn to his performance in Situation B, only four days later, we find that a solution must be worked out almost anew. Note, however, the skill and precision with which the broom was finally used—an indication of complete insight.

Introspection lends support to the likelihood that varying degrees of insight may accompany a solution and that the latter may affect insight qualitatively and quantitatively. H. G. Wyatt, in his analysis of Ruger's and Peterson's experiments, works out a somewhat similar gradation of insight, without, however, showing its relation to the solution:

"The moment or act of insight can only sometimes be described as a sudden flash; it is often a succession of glimmering apprehensions and is found in all degrees, from elusive and indefinite dimness to a clear and convincing definiteness." [7]

[7] Wyatt, H. G., "Intelligence in Man and Ape." *Psychological Review,* September, 1926, p. 375.

With further reference to solutions with *sudden* insight, it should be pointed out that these may also be of two kinds: on the one hand, we have the emergence of insight while the subject is on the scene of action, as in Cases 18 and 21, referred to on page 39; and, on the other hand, insight is functionally ready at the beginning of a new exposure, following one or more unsuccessful experiences in preceding exposures, as though it had matured between exposures. Case 10, II-C, is illustrative of this type of solution, of which a more detailed analysis will be undertaken in the section on Comparative Data, Chapter V. For the time being the discussion of Types of Solution may be concluded with the following classification:

1. Solution with *Immediate* Insight.
2. Solution with *Gradual* Insight.
   A. *Partial* Insight.
   B. *Complete* Insight.
3. Solution with *Sudden* Insight.
   A. Matured *during* exposure.
   B. Matured *between* exposures.

Table II-A pictures each individual with reference to Solutions, and Table II-B gives the frequency for each Solution Type.

As in the case of the Response, so here we find that the Solution fits the situation (though the relationship is not the same). Thus the Immediate Solution is most frequent in Situations B and C of Series I and in Situation B of Series II, which follow most closely the pattern of the key-situations of each series. The corollary is also equally true here. That is, the subject does not favor any one type of solution but may run through all six (including Failure) on the nine test-situations.

There seems to be a tendency for one failure to be followed by further failures, pointing to a probable transfer of "attitude," which is confirmed by personal observation. The increased difficulty of subsequent situations is undoubtedly an additional factor in explanation of this tendency.

TRANSFER AND RETENTION

Attention may well be called here to the all-but-perfect transfer (one exception) of the principle involved in the key-situations of each Series to Test-Situations B and C of Series I and

B of Series II. As has already been stated in the preceding chapter, we propose to consider Transfer and Retention—the ability to retain the principle involved in the solution—as Secondary Criteria of Insight, not only of the presence of Insight but also of the degree to which it is present, that is, whether Partial or Complete.

Thorndike would have been willing to concede reasoned behavior or inference (hence insight) to the cats in his puzzle-box experiments if the time-curves had showed a sudden and permanent drop.[8] The Immediate Solutions in Situations B and C of Series I and in Situation B of Series II are equivalent to such a drop in the time-curve. As is seen in Table II-B, there are for these situations 60 Immediate Solutions out of a total of 71 possible solutions, that is, 84.5 per cent.[9]

The remaining ten solutions and one failure deserve a further analysis which will also serve to better establish the relation between Insight and Transfer. For this purpose the reader is referred to Table II-A.

1. Case 7—The absence of an Immediate Solution in I-B is preceded by a solution with Partial Insight in I-A.

2. Case 7—The absence of an Immediate Solution in II-B is preceded by a solution with Partial Insight in II-A.

3. Case 12—Failure in I-C is preceded by a solution with Complete Insight in I-A and I-B, but the subject's tendency to daydream often absorbs her interest and attention to the exclusion of all else.

4. Case 35—The absence of an Immediate Solution in I-C is preceded by solutions with Complete Insight in I-A and I-B, but this subject's activity was always found to vary markedly with her "mood" and for this situation she was particularly lethargic and querulous.

5. Case 31—The absence of an Immediate Solution in I-C is preceded by solutions with Complete Insight in I-A and I-B but for this situation the subject was in an obstreperous, reckless mood, with a tendency to try out the least likely devices before turning to the well-established method.

6. Case 14—The absence of an Immediate Solution in II-B is preceded by a solution with Partial Insight in II-A.

[8] Thorndike, E. L., *Op. cit.*

[9] This is by no means an adequate discussion of the time factor as it applies to Thorndike's experiments, but will suffice for the present purpose.

TABLE II-A

Types of Solution in Individual Cases

Case No.	Sex	Age	Series I — Test-Situations					Age	Series II — Test-Situations			
			A	B	C	D	E		A	B	C	D
1	B	3–3	S–B	I	I	G–C	G–C	3–4	I	I	S–D	G–C
2	G	3–2	I	I	I	S–D	G–C	3–4	S–D	I	S–D	S–D
3	B	3–3	S–D	I	I	G–C	F	3–5	S–D	I	G–C	F
7	G	2–6	G–P	S–D	I	F	F	2–9	G–P	S–D	G–C	F
10	B	2–9	S–B	I	I	G–P	F	3–0	S–D	I	S–B	F
11	G	2–8	S–B	I	t	G–P	F	2–10	I	I	I	F
12	G	2–5	S–B	I	F	F	F	2–7	G–C	I	F	F
14	B	4–1	S–D	I	I	I	G–C	4–3	S–D	S–D	G–C	S–D
15	B	3–3	I	I		I	I	3–5	S–D	I	G–C	S–D
21	B	3–6	S–D	I	I	G–C	S–D	3–8	S–D	I		S–D
27	B	3–3	S–B	I	I	F	F	3–5	I	I	G–C	F
28	B	3–2	S–D	I	I	G–P	S–B	3–4	I	I	I	F
35	G	1–11	S–D	I	G–C	F	F	2–3	G–C	I	F	G–C
41	B	2–11	I	I	I	I	S–B	3–4	G–C	G–C	I	G–C
42	B	2–8	G–C	I	I	G–C	S–D	3–1	S–D	I	G–C	G–C
43	G	2–8	I	I	I	F	F	3–2	G–C	I	I	F
4	G	2–11	S–D	I	I	I	F	3–4	F			
5	B	2–10	F					3–0	G–P	G–C	G–C	S–D
6	G	3–2	F					3–5	F			
8	G	2–4	G–C	I		I	G–C	F 2–7	F			
9	G	3–1	F					3–4	G–C	I	G–C	F
13	G	3–10	I	I	I		G–C	4–1	F			
16	G	3–8	F					3–9	F			
17	G	2–7	F					2–10	F			
20	G	3–8	F					3–9	F			
19	G	1–7	F						Not used for		this	Series
22	B	3–4	F					3–6	F			
23	G	3–4	F					3–6	G–C	I	G–P	S–D
24	G	3–8	S–B	I	I	F	F	3–9	F			
25	G	2–4	F					2–5	F			
26	G	2–1	F					2–2	F			
29	G	2–6	F					2–9	I	I	S–D	F
30	B	3–10	F					4–1	G–C	I	G–C	G–C
31	B	2–11	I	I	G–C	F	G–C	3–3	S–D	Left	school	
32	G	2–3	F						Not used for		this	Series
33	G	2–8	S–D	I	I	S–D	F	3–0	F			
34	G		Not used for		this	Series		2–0	G–P	G–C	F	F
36	B	1–11	F					2–5	G–P	G–C	G–P	G–P
37	G	1–11	F						Left	school		
38	B		Not used for		this	Series		2–6	F			
39	B		Not used for		this	Series		2–3	G–P	G–C	F	F
40	G	2–10	F					3–4	S–D	I	I	G–C
44	G		Not used for		this	Series		2–8	I	I	F	F
18	G	3–8	S–D	I	I	S–D	S–D	3–9	F			

Note: The symbols S–D, S–B, G–P, G–C, and I stand for the five Types of Solution described on pages 39 ff. Sudden Insight matured during exposure, Sudden Insight matured between exposures, Partial Insight and Complete Insight, gradually matured, and Immediate Solution. F stands for failure at the end of five trials; where it occurs in the key-situation of a Series, the subject is dropped from the Series.

TABLE II-B

FREQUENCY OF TYPES OF SOLUTION

Solution Type	Series I Test-Situations					Total	Series II Test-Situations				Total	Both Series Total
	A	B	C	D	E		A	B	C	D		
I	6	22	19	4	1	52	6	19	5	0	30	82
G–P	1	0	0	3	0	4	5	0	2	1	8	12
G–C	2	0	2	5	5	14	7	5	9	6	27	41
S–D	8	1	0	3	3	15	9	2	3	6	20	35
S–B	6	0	0	0	2	8	0	0	1	0	1	9
F	17	0	1	7	12	37	14	0	5	13	32	69
No. of Cases	40	23	22	22	23		41	26	25	26		

NOTE: The symbols used in this table represent the same terms as in Table II-A.

7. Case 41—The absence of an Immediate Solution in II-B is preceded by a solution with Complete Insight in II-A, which was evolved, however, with great difficulty. In fact, this is one of the rare cases where an ambiguous inhibition toward the stick, displayed by several children (to which further reference will be made later) is overcome. The subject struggled with this situation in a manly fashion for four exposures and one success was apparently not sufficient to overcome all the irrelevant associations left by the struggle.

8. Case 5—The absence of an Immediate Solution in II-B is preceded by a solution with Partial Insight in II-A. This case is cited in Chapter II, page 11.

9. Case 34—The absence of an Immediate Solution in II-B is preceded by a solution with Partial Insight in II-A.

10. Case 36—The absence of an Immediate Solution in II-B is preceded by a solution with Partial Insight in II-A.

11. Case 39—The absence of an Immediate Solution in II-B is preceded by a solution with Partial Insight in II-A. This case is cited in Chapter II, page 23.

Of the eleven cases showing an absence of Immediate Solutions in I-B and I-C and in II-B, six subjects solved the preceding key-situation with Partial Insight and the other five cases can be adequately explained on other grounds. This linkage between interference with transfer and solutions with Partial Insight in the key-situations constitutes a fairly strong case for Transfer as a criterion of İnsight.

Retention of the principle involved in solutions, as shown by the marked falling off of the Primitive Response (see Tables I-B and I-C) in situations subsequent to the key-situation is closely allied to Transfer, and what was shown with regard to the latter is equally true of the former. But the validity of these criteria can be ascertained by an investigation specifically designed for the purpose.

In the Ruger experiments referred to above, "transfer of training" also presupposed understanding or insight.

CHANCE

Thus far we have seen that a solution is accompanied by Partial or by Complete Insight, the latter being far more common—12:137—(see Table II-B, Solution Types I, G-C, S-P, and S-B as against G-P). Though this automatically rules out chance solutions as such, that is, solutions unaccompanied by insight (with possible exceptions, to be superlatively cautious, among the twelve solutions with Partial Insight), it does not rule out the factor of chance in solutions. The question may still be asked: what part does chance play in facilitating a solution? The following illustrations help to answer this question:

Case 36, Boy, 28 mos., I-E, third exposure, 5′: Subject glanced at the suspended doll and ran off for the green block which he shoved over directly under the objective and then continued to shove it around in an aimless manner. [This tended to become an intoxicating procedure with this subject; so Experimenter diverted him.] (3′) Experimenter urged him to try again at which he placed the block under the objective, looked up and said "Doll too high"; *picked up green block and placed it on top of the grocery box* and then began to run around.

This subject's activity is of a random, obstreperous, distracted nature, as favorable to chance solutions as it is unfavorable to an awareness of his activity. Thus, an excellent clue, the very key to the solution, goes astray, and is not recaptured at subsequent exposures.

Case 39, Boy, 29 mos., II-D, second exposure, 4′ 45″: Whined and said "No, No," but in 45 seconds picked up both sticks, examined them at both ends, and tried to fit them; (1′ 35″) *succeeded in joining them* and was very happy with the lengthened stick; (2′ 15″) tried to walk out of the pen and then began to wave the stick around outside the pen, with no apparent intention toward objective.

Third exposure, 3′: Subject reached for objective with his hand over the top of the pen, whining; (40″) reached with both sticks held in one hand, whining, "I can't"; (1′) threw one stick away and stuck his finger in the hole of the other, looking at Experimenter; picked up the other stick, *fitted the two and said, "See big stick";* played with it, waving it around outside, but making no attempt to reach objective.

Fourth exposure, 4′: Subject reached over the top of the pen with his hand; picked up the sticks and examined them carefully; (1′ 15″) *joined the sticks and began* fitting the long stick between the bars; (2′ 30″) looked at objective and said, "Can't reach it. Where is the stick? All gone," looking around for it; (1′) again fitted the stick between the bars.

This test situation remains unsolved, though the wherewithal is in the subject's hand.

Case 33, Girl, 36 mos., II-A, first exposure, 4′ 30″: Subject tried to get out then began reaching for objective with her hand between the bars; (45″) picked up the stick and said, "Here's a stick"; put it down and began playing "house." Subject leaned over—"out of the window"—and tried again to reach the objective, saying, "I can't; put it over here," and continued with her game, ignoring the objective. (3′) Experimenter urged her to try again, at which she tried to reach it with her hands, by pushing her feet out between the spaces and by leaning over, repeating, "I can't."

Second exposure, 5′: Subject sat still, looking at the doll outside the pen; (30″) said, "I can't," but leaned over, trying to reach it and made other attempts; walked off but (1′ 30″) began to reach as before; (2′) grasped the stick and dropped it outside the pen, then picked it up and placed it touching the doll; picked the stick up and said, "See, I can get the stick"; shoved the doll away with the stick and *continued to use it merely as a toy;* (4′ 30″) tried to reach it with her hand through the bars.

Third exposure, 6′: Subject talked to the toy-dog outside the pen; (40″) tried to reach by pushing her leg through the space, wailing, "I can't get it"; (50″) turned around, saw the stick and quickly put it up on the molding extension at the back of the pen, going through the motions of piano-playing on it; came back for a look at objective and (1′ 45″) turned sharply toward the stick and said, "I can get it," meaning the stick; picked it up and played with it, close to the objective; made a game of touching objective with the stick, dropping it outside and then recapturing it.

The same activity is repeated in the next two exposures but no solution is achieved. Though the stick and objective are often found in an optimum arrangement, this fact in itself is not sufficient to yield a solution.

Case 5, Boy, 36 mos., II-D, first exposure, 6′ 30″: Subject reached for objective with the stick through the space; (25″) examined the stick and reached with it again; (1′) tried with the other stick in the same way; moved it out as far as it would go and then brought it back with the other stick; (2′) looked at Experimenter and then tried to reach for objective over the top of the pen and again through the space; (2′ 45″) examined the sticks; (3′) tried to reach objective through the space again, stretching to the utmost; (3′ 45″) changed sticks and shoved one with the other cautiously toward the objective; (5′ 15″) reached over the top as before; (5′ 30″) *caught his finger in the hole at* one end of the stick and (5′ 40″) joined the sticks and secured the objective.

The mere chance catching of the finger in the hole suggested the complete and immediate solution. It is interesting to contrast with this case the following cases:

Case 3, Boy, 41 mos., II-D, second exposure, 4′ 45″: Subject reached for objective through the space with his hand, saying, "It's way over there"; (45″) examined the stick and said, "This is a big stick"; (1′) tried to reach objective with it over the top; continued to reach but indifferently, examining the stick while doing so and playing with it; (3′) *stuck his finger in the hole* at end of stick. (3′ 30″) Reached for objective as before.

The activity is practically the same during the next three exposures, the subject continues to examine the sticks but gets no further. There are four other subjects who reach this step and stop there, fixated, as it were, on the level to which chance had brought them.

Case 44, Girl, 33 mos., II-D, first exposure, 4′: Subject reached for objective with her hand through the space; (30″) examined the sticks and stuck her finger in the hole; (1′) amused herself by fitting the sticks between the bars; (2′) *tried to fit the sticks together* but at the wrong ends and began to reach for objective with both sticks; (2′ 45″) began walking around, using the sticks as canes; (3′ 15″) tried again to reach objective over the top of the pen.

The subsequent four exposures represent a regression from this level. The subject does not again try to join the sticks, nor even to examine them. There are two other cases who reach the level of trying to join the sticks, without getting any further.

Case 9, Girl, 28 mos., II-D, fourth exposure, 5′ 30″: Subject reached for objective with the stick over the top of the pen, finally dropping it outside; picked up other stick and dropped it outside, then amused herself by reaching for the sticks with her leg through the space; (3′) looked at the opening at end of stick and tried to join the sticks but without success; (4′) reached for objective with one stick and again tried to join the sticks; *succeeded* and was delighted with the long stick, *paying no attention to the objective;* took the sticks apart.

Second exposure, 3′: Subject reached for objective with the stick through the space, saying, "I'll get the beads to-day"; tried to reach them over the top, and then began to bang with the stick; (1′) examined the end of the stick and picked up the other stick, trying to join both; this done, she carried the long stick aloft, saying, "Big stick"; (2′) took sticks apart and used them as canes.

This subject, as well as Case 39, has gone the whole length. The sticks are joined but they are used as things in themselves, as toys, and not with reference to the whole field, thereby leaving the problem unsolved.

It is clear from these illustrations that chance alone is ineffectual in problem-situations of this type. Even in Ruger's experiments,[10] some of which favor chance solutions, we find that though possible variations in the solving process mostly come

TABLE III

FREQUENCY OF TYPES OF RESPONSE IN SOLUTIONS

PRIMITIVE RESPONSE

Series	Test-Situation	Solution Types						Total Suc.*	Total F.*	Total G–I*	Total S–I*
		I	G–P	G–C	S–D	S–B	F				
I	A	5	0	0	4	4	14				
	B	9	0	0	0	0	0				
	C	3	0	0	0	0	1				
	D	0	0	0	1	0	3				
	E	0	0	0	0	0	5	26	23	0	9
II	A	1	1	1	2	0	9				
	B	0	0	4	1	0	0				
	C	0	0	1	0	0	2				
	D	0	0	0	0	0	1	11	12	9	3
Total		18	1	6	8	4	35	37 (21%)	35 (51%)	9	12

[10] Ruger, H. A., *The Psychology of Efficiency.* Archives of Psychology, No. 15, June, 1910.

TABLE III (*Continued*)

RANDOM RESPONSE

Series	Test Situation	Solution Types						Total Suc.*	Total F.*	Total G–I *	Total S–I *
		I	G–P	G–C	S–D	S–B	F				
I	A	0	0	0	1	1	0	2	0	0	2
				Consistently 0 for the rest of this Series							
II	A	1	1	1	1	0	1				
	B	0	0	0	0	0	0				
	C	0	0	0	1	0	1				
	D	1	0	0	1	0	1	7	3	2	4
Total		2	1	1	4	1	3	9 (5%)	3 (4%)	2	6

EXPLORATION AND ELIMINATION

Series	Test Situation	Solution Types						Total Suc.*	Total F.*	Total G–I *	Total S–I *
		I	G–P	G–C	S–D	S–B	F				
I	A	0	1	2	3	0	2				
	B	0	0	0	1	0	0				
	C	1	0	2	0	0	0				
	D	0	3	5	2	0	4				
	E	0	0	5	3	2	7	30	13	19	11
II	A	1	4	5	6	0	1				
	B	1	0	1	1	0	0				
	C	1	1	8	2	0	2				
	D	0	1	6	5	0	11	43	14	27	13
Total		4	10	34	23	2	27	73 (41%)	27 (39%)	46	24

* Suc. stands for Success; F. for Failure; G–I for Gradual Insight (both P and C); S–I for Sudden Insight (both D and B).

Percentages where given should be read in terms of total number of successes (179) and failures (69).

Caution: The reader must not expect to derive the total number of successes and failures from this table, since Immediate Solutions that are not preceded by any other Response (see page 32) are not given here. For actual totals of successes and failures, see Table II-B.

by chance, their value is realized in direct proportion to the *conscious attention* and *analysis accorded them.* Here, as elsewhere, analysis is intimately associated with insight. Koffka [11] agrees with Ruger that insight may come "through the *employment* of chance."

[11] Koffka, K., *The Growth of the Mind.* Harcourt, Brace & Co., 1925.

To sum up this question of the rôle of chance in solutions, it may therefore be said that chance may be instrumental in bringing about an optimum constellation of the elements of a problem-situation, and that this constellation may or may not arouse insight. But unless insight is aroused, the most favorable constellation may go astray and the problem remain unsolved, as in the cases recorded above.

Before the discussion of the solution is closed, the reader's attention is called to Table III, which gives a composite picture of each Type of Response with reference to the Solution.

1. The Primitive Response is seen to yield about as many successes as failures, and in terms of percentages, a far greater proportion of failures.

2. Exploration and Elimination, on the other hand, distinctly favors successes, which are almost three times as frequent as failures. This ratio becomes more significant in the light of the fact that the Exploration and Elimination Response occurs most frequently in the more difficult test-situations, as was seen in Table I-C.

3. The Primitive Response seems to lead most often to the Immediate Solution, the cause of which fact is probably the prepotency of the Primitive Response, rather than any inherent relation between it and the Immediate Solution.

4. Exploration and Elimination Response seems to favor solutions with Gradual Insight, when considered alone, but when compared to other types of Response, it is most often associated with solutions with Sudden Insight. It must, of course, be borne in mind that Table II-B shows Exploration and Elimination to be the most common type of Response.

5. Nothing can be said of the Random Response because of the infrequency of its occurrence.

CHAPTER V

COMPARATIVE DATA

Because of the fact that Köhler's experimental work was limited to nine apes only it is impossible to derive quantitative indices of comparison between their performance and that of the children who served as subjects for this investigation. The comparative data must therefore be limited to qualitative facts which, it is hoped, will nevertheless throw some light upon striking similarities or dissimilarities in the behavior of apes and children when confronted with the same (objectively speaking) problem-situations.

TYPES OF RESPONSE

The Primitive Response.—This is as prominent with apes as with children, being in both cases the characteristic initial response. The outstretched arm is, however, accompanied by the upward leap in the former instead of the tiptoe position in the latter. "All six apes vainly endeavored to reach their objective by leaping up from the ground," arm outstretched (as indicated by the illustrations); and "Tschego first tries to reach the fruit with her hand." [1] Similarly for the other apes in Series II-A. Not only is the Primitive Response the initial response, but, as with the children, it is also resorted and reverted to temporarily in a dilemma, as the most familiar thing to do. Thus in the absence of a stick, or when failing to see it, or when its use is momentarily forgotten, the apes will try to reach the objective with their hands through the bars just as the children do. Similarly for both, the Primitive Response becomes less and less frequent as the use of "tools" becomes more familiar.

The Random Response.—This is relatively as infrequent with apes as with children, though somewhat more common among the former and of a more violent nature, anger at being thwarted playing an active part. The outstanding difference, however, is

[2] Köhler, W., *The Mentality of Apes.* Harcourt, Brace & Co., 1925.

not only in degree but also in kind. Whereas the ape's anger is more often vented in a purely destructive manner, in no way calculated to bring the objective within reach, the child's resentment expresses itself in activity directed at the objective, whether it be the toy or release from confinement (the pen), and is therefore constructive in nature. Compare for this purpose the accounts of Case 18, I-A and Case 39, II-A given in Chapter II with the following: "The box he [Koko] merely frequently stared at in a peculiar manner. Suddenly he flew at it and began a violent attack: he was beside himself with rage, flung the box to and fro, and kicked it. These outbreaks . . . were now concentrated entirely upon the box." [2] It is, however, true of both apes and children that "under the influence of strong, unsatisfied emotion, the animal must do something in the spatial direction in which the object of his emotion is situated. He must somehow get into touch with this objective, . . . even if it is only to hurl the movables in his cage towards it." [3] Witness the throwing of the stick at the objective after many futile attempts to reach, in Case 42, II-D, Chapter II; and Sultan's performance: "His hunger increased; he seized twigs and pushed them toward his coveted prize; finally, he threw them, pebbles, blades of grass, and all available movable objects at the fruit." [4]

An additional difference is seen in the fact that the Random Response occurs with children either at the outset of the experiment or after unsuccessful attempts to reach the objective and with apes only in the latter case. This is probably due to the fact that the pen situation is more objectionable and more novel to the children than is the cage for the apes.

Exploration and Elimination.—This type of Response is the most frequent with apes, as it is with children, but it is often characterized by greater variety and ingenuity in the case of the former. This is undoubtedly due first to the fact that the apes were tested in a setting less fixed than that in which the children were tested. For example, in addition to the stick or box of a given problem-situation, ropes, blankets, iron bars, tables, etc., would often be lying around as part of the furniture

[2] Köhler, W., *Op. cit.*, p. 45.
[3] *Ibid.*, p. 93.
[4] *Ibid.*, p. 92.

of the apes' dwelling place in which they were tested. These stray articles were frequently introduced by the apes in the solving process. In the second place, the apes are superlatively strong and exceedingly fine gymnasts as compared with children so that they could and did try to reach the objective by means outside the physical range of children, as scaling a wall, or vaulting up a pole, or detaching a firmly fixed object, as a shoe-scraper, to reach with in lieu of a stick. Exploration with Partial Insight of the complete field occurs in about the same proportion among apes as among children. Sultan's maneuvers in the two-box experiment (I-E) are illustrative of this type of response.[5]

As with the children, so with the apes, Exploration and Elimination is often abandoned for the Primitive or Random Response when the subject is fatigued or at the end of his mental resources or disinterested. It is equally true of apes that no one Response is favored exclusively by one subject but that it conforms to the requirements of the total situation; and that no Response is to be regarded as a definite, decisive act, but rather as a part of a continuous stream of action, the solving process. The labeling of these parts as types of response is necessarily an artificial affair. To be sure, the solving process tends to become more stabilized with continued experimentation and the consequent elimination of the Primitive and Random Responses (see Tables I-A, B, C), but is thoroughly so only when accompanied by complete insight, that is, when it becomes the solution itself.

TYPES OF SOLUTION

The Immediate Solution.—This does not occur in key-situations among apes as it does among children, but is confined to Situations B and C of Series I and Situation B of Series II. Nor does it invariably occur in these situations. It is impossible to determine how the frequency of the Immediate Solution in these situations compares for the two types of subjects, though it is probably higher for children, since an ape's solution is often delayed by his difficulty in seeing the connection between stick or box and objective unless these are so placed that he can see both at the same time.

[5] Köhler, W., *Op. cit.*, p. 48.

If the experimenter takes care that the stick is not visible to the animal when gazing directly at the objective—and that, vice versa, a direct look at the stick excludes the whole region of the objective from the field of vision—then, generally speaking, recourse to this instrument is either prevented or at least greatly retarded, even when it has already been frequently used.[6]

Though this handicap is to some degree true of children in the key-situations, it is not all true in subsequent ones, when they have become familiar with the use of "tools." Here it no longer matters in the least whether the child is looking at the stick or box and objective at the same time or not and most often it does not so confront them. This points to a higher level of transfer and retention in the child, while the absence of Immediate Solutions by apes in the key-situations indicates either a lower level of mental development or a narrower range of experience.

Solution with Gradual Insight.—This is perhaps the most frequent type of solution among apes, whereas the Immediate Solution is most frequent for children. Gradual solutions with partial insight are absent except for the problem of statics in the building experiment (I-E). It is significant that this problem barely exists for children. The stability of the structure offers no difficulty once the idea of the structure is grasped. Only in three cases was the grocery box placed on top of the smaller block, and this structure would have been sufficiently stable had not the open side of the grocery box faced the floor, thus engulfing the smaller block! This was hailed by all three subjects as a huge joke and led in one case to the more foolish procedure of piling the green block on a corner of the open face of the grocery box, with the natural result that the block fell into the grocery box. By this time the subject was too hilarious to proceed intelligently. In fact, it seemed to the experimenter that the second error of judgment would not have occurred if the subject had not already been partly demoralized by the first mishap. In the second case the subject automatically mounted the pseudo-structure and reached up for the objective, as though under compulsion to carry out to completion the course of action originally undertaken. In the third case further exploration and elimination followed but not in building.

[6] Köhler, W., *Op. cit.*, p. 38.

With the exception of these three cases, building presents no problem to the children, even those as young as two years and eight months (though Koffka places this achievement at the end of the third year),[7] and in no case is the problem as serious as it is for the apes:

Here are two problems: the one (put the second box up) is not really a difficult task for the animals, provided they know the use to which boxes can be put; the other (add one box to the other, so that it stays there firmly, making the whole thing higher) is extremely difficult . . . In the latter case a limited body of special shape is to be brought into contact with another one like it, in such a way that a particular result is obtained; and this is where the chimpanzee seems to reach the limit of his capacity.[8]

The child appears to be nowhere near the limit of his capacity with regard to this point.

The ease with which a perfectly good idea, in fact the solution itself, is abandoned, (and sometimes never again returned to) if not followed by attainment of the goal, as in two of the cases cited above and in Case 1, II-C, Chapter II, deserves further mention. This is as characteristic of apes as of children, and bears witness to the fact that for both types of subjects insight may occur unaccompanied or only partially accompanied by consciousness, in which case it is of a fleeting and unstable nature unless reinforced by a practical success. This is further borne out by adult introspection.

With further reference to solutions with Partial Insight, it may be noted that though there is no positive evidence that such solutions occur among apes except in the problem of statics, occasional difficulties in Situations B and C of Series I and Situation B of Series II point to the probability that they do. At any rate, the twelve instances of such solutions among children, already discussed on page 40, furnish sufficient grounds for believing that solutions may be accompanied by varying degrees of insight.

Solutions with Sudden Insight.—This occurs quite commonly but there seems to be no instance of insight maturing away from the field of action and being suddenly employed when the animal is confronted with the situation afresh. It is not quite clear from Köhler's account whether the chimpanzee is incapable of

[7] Koffka, K., *Op. cit.*, p. 306.
[8] Köhler, W., *Op. cit.*, p. 152.

delayed solutions of this type, though this seems highly probable in view of the difficulty he experiences in keeping objective and tool in mind together when the two are not physically in connection. Of course it is not at all certain what passes in the child's mind during the interval between repeated failures and the exposure at which the solution with sudden insight occurs and what relation it bears to this solution: whether the child copes with a mental image of the situation while away from the actual situation; or whether the interval merely serves to clear the subject's mind of all associations and assumptions relating to the problem so that he is enabled to see the elements of the situation in their proper relation at the next exposure; or whether the child has received aid from an adult during the interval.

Ruger regards the second explanation as more applicable to his cases of "fixed assumptions" which, he finds, were often broken up by just an interval after which the puzzle would be solved almost immediately upon coming back to it.[9]

Miss Heidbreder, however, finds that the concept of straight and curved lines, upon which her problem-situations hinge, occurred to her adult subjects in subsequent trials, not as if they "saw them in the situation but as if they thought of them 'as impressions from the past.' "[10] She calls this phenomenon summation and it is not unlike what probably happens in the case of the child if the first explanation is accepted. Adult introspection recognizes both possibilities; it is probable that both are operative in the child as well. There is no direct evidence of either experience in the chimpanzee. In other respects the solution with Sudden Insight occurs similarly as with children, characterized by the same spectacular, climactic appearance.

The third possibility that the child received aid from an adult between exposures is unlikely for several reasons: first, the child prattles naïvely throughout the exposure about all sorts of things and it is more than probable that it would betray the fact in one way or another that it had received assistance; second, some situations in which such solutions occur are so complicated as to preclude the possibility that a child of two to four years could describe them accurately enough to permit of constructive and

[9] Ruger, H. A., *The Psychology of Efficiency*, p. 29. Archives of Psychology, No. 15, June, 1910.

[10] Heidbreder, E., *An Experimental Study of Thinking*, p. 73. Archives of Psychology, 1924.

specific aid from an adult. The situation described in Case 10, II-C, page 14, is such, as is also Situation I-E in which two such solutions occur.

There is but one instance where aid was actually given to a child, in Situation II-A, the simplest of the series and under unique circumstances. This Case is cited fully in Chapter II and discussed with regard to this incident on page 61.

CHANCE

What has been said with regard to the rôle of chance in solutions with children as subjects is equally true of apes. Though it may aid in solutions, it does so only if it serves to arouse insight. Thus, chance may have favored an optimum position of the two bamboo sticks for Sultan but insight was essential not only to help him realize that the position was optimum (which is a problem in itself), but also to see the relation of the lengthened stick to the rest of the field.[11] It should be emphasized that what has been said of chance applies only to situations such as were used for this investigation; that in situations approximating the wire-puzzle or puzzle-box type it may be the sole agent in a solution. Thus the subject, by continued random manipulation of a wire-puzzle, may actually cause it to fall apart, much to his surprise; or the cat, excitedly dashing around in the puzzle-box, may accidentally hit against the device which holds the door, thereby releasing it. These acts are solutions in an objective sense primarily, subjective only to the extent that such an experience can be utilized in subsequent solutions. And the extent to which this can be done is commensurate with the degree of insight accompanying the solution.

FAILURES

An analysis of solutions in terms of insight should logically be followed by an analysis of failures in the same terms. To say, however, that these are due to an absence of insight is to state only a partial truth that has not even the merit of being a fundamental one. There are grounds for believing that failures may occur even where insight is present, and the question inevitably arises: What factors prevent the arousal of insight and its natural consummation in a practical success?

[11] Köhler, W., *Op. cit.*, p. 131 ff.

The answer to this question is perforce tentative and speculative, based as it is upon subjective observations. There can be no doubt, however, that the following factors, submitted as responsible individually or in combination for the partial or complete inhibition of insight, do affect the solving process.

1. *Self-Consciousness.*—Unable as the self-conscious subject is to lose himself, the attention directed to the problem is necessarily at a lower level. The uneasiness which is a natural concomitant of self-consciousness prevents the subject from carefully surveying the field. He is disinclined to commit himself to action lest it result in failure, of which he is afraid and ashamed. Such an emotional state imposes so many motor inhibitions, not to mention the mental inhibitions, that even where insight is present it is prevented from consummating in action. Thus in Case 5-I, cited in Chapter II, there can be no doubt that the subject entertains some hypothesis with regard to the block but this is not acted upon, because of the inhibiting force exerted by self-consciousness. Case 16, also cited in Chapter II, is a perfect illustration of the "self-attentive attitude," which Ruger found, in combination with "emotional tension, embarrassment, and self-consciousness" to be a prominent factor affecting the appearance of variations (and therefore of solutions) in the solving process of his subjects.[12] Failure in five cases may be referred to this factor.

2. *Lack of Confidence.*—This is generally found in combination with a general timidity and a need for adult approval and is given freer play in the presence of the experimenter. The subject prefaces all action with a look at the experimenter—manifestly a plea for approval or encouragement—and is inclined to interpret the absence of a response as disapproval or permission withheld. It is impossible to say in how many cases a flash of insight—as when the subject looks significantly at the objective, then at the box, and again at the objective, ending with an appealing look at the experimenter—is kept from maturing into a solution, on account of lack of self-confidence, but there is sufficient evidence to prove that such cases do occur. There are, in the first place, authentic reports of children as young as sixteen and seventeen months reaching for inaccessible yet desired objects by means of chairs, boxes, satchels (Preyer's

12 Ruger, H. A., *Op. cit.*, p. 16.

son), spoon (Mrs. Moore's baby thirty-six weeks' old!), whereas the youngest child to solve the first situation was twenty-three months. Undoubtedly the fact that in these cases the problem arises spontaneously—originates with the child rather than being suggested to it—favors a greater display of initiative in so far as it implies a higher level of attention functioning in the solving process. It is significant that problems which are so closely related to the child's everyday experiences may yet appear as artificial to him and therefore fail to elicit a maximum response.

Ruger's need to screen himself from some of his adult subjects whose attitude is so "submissive" or "suggestible" as to interpret every chance gesture, change in posture and look on the part of the experimenter as a clue for their solutions, is a recognition of the inhibiting effect of lack of confidence upon solutions.

Köhler also found it necessary on occasions to withdraw behind a screen, not because his subjects, the chimpanzees, are lacking in self-confidence, but because they too tend to rely upon the experimenter, and any such reliance interferes with the maturing of insight in that it directs attention away from the field of action, i.e., the problem.

This procedure was not followed in this investigation, first because it would have interfered with the constancy of objective conditions, and second, because it was felt that the withdrawal of the experimenter would have only substituted one emotional disturbance for another.

Failure in eight cases can be accounted for by a lack of confidence and its concomitants.

3. *"Fixations"*.—It is a truism that a problem is approached by a subject with a certain "mind set," even with certain assumptions, that further assumptions are formed with regard to it during the solving process, but to the extent to which we permit any one assumption to usurp our attention to the exclusion of all others, we lessen the chances of seeing the problem in the right perspective and therefore of gaining insight into the problem. Thus Ruger found that his subjects were often rendered insensitive to variations by becoming too devoted to certain assumptions, no matter how accidentally adopted. He found, however, that these assumptions were often broken up by a fresh start, as on a new trial.[13]

[13] Ruger, H. A., *Op. cit.*, p. 16.

We have termed "fixations" a phenomenon which is probably similar in kind to Ruger's "fixed assumptions" though different in degree. In all of the eleven cases which fall into this class of failures, the assumption became so fixed as not to be broken up during the five exposures. In all of these cases the assumption, whatever its exact content, involves the stick or the block. The one or the other certainly loses its neutrality for the subject and compels his attention. Where the assumption is of a specific nature, as in Case 18, Chapter II, the stick or block will be significantly looked at but not touched. Where the assumption is more vague, an ill-defined suspicion, then it compels not only the subject's attention but an explicit discharge of energy in the direction of the suspected object. Thus the subject will perhaps shift the position of the stick or kick it gently, but whatever is done to the object tends to become a stereotyped act, repeated, as though it were a ritual, at subsequent exposures. The subject often shows signs of uneasiness until this detail is attended to. Cases 9, 13, and 26 will give the reader some idea of what happens. These are intentionally recorded not too objectively, so that the reader may not miss all of what he would have caught in a picture or from a personal observation.

A further analysis of this phenomenon must of necessity be speculative. Judging from the complete behavioristic picture so often repeated, it would seem that these "fixations" are, at least in some cases, started off by a vague suspicion or "hunch" with regard to the stick or block (as judged by the significant series of looks at the object, the experimenter, and the objective). This suspicion renders the subject uneasy, upsets his "equilibrium," a state somewhat alleviated by a discharge of energy, preferably and most naturally in the direction of the suspected object. Thus the block is sat upon or the stick is moved. But whatever the act, it may be regarded as in the general direction of "closure" as the Gestalt psychologists would have it, or "satisfaction" in Thorndike's terminology. Judging by the subject's unmistakable uneasiness, it is fair to assume that the act takes place in an emotional setting which, of course, helps it to become intrenched in the subject's mind. When the situation is again faced at a subsequent trial the same uneasiness is probably experienced, and what is more natural than that it should be relieved in the same way, by repeating the only familiar feature of the situation? Thus it is that so many subjects become "fixated" or "conditioned" to a particular bit of behavior with regard to the stick or block. Once the block or stick becomes the core of a "fixation," the chances for insight or a solution are practically nil.

That an "assumption" may sometimes be of a more specific nature than is indicated by the above analysis, is borne out by Case 18. This subject solved all the problem-situations of Series I promptly and intelligently but failed to solve Situation A of Series II at the end of five exposures, merely looking in the direction of the stick and appearing very much distressed over her failure. The writer later learned from the subject's mother that it even disturbed her sleep. Questioning the mother further, the experimenter learned that the child had been in the habit of riding astride a yardstick at home, much to the annoyance of her mother who used it constantly for her work. The child was forbidden to use the yardstick. When, about the same time, she complained to her mother that she could not reach the "doll outside the little house" at school, her mother asked whether there was anything inside the house with which to reach, whereupon the child answered explosively, "Yes, a yardstick"! The ordinary stick used in this situation was actually of about the same proportions as a yardstick which apparently had for the child but one association, *Verboten*.

That associations or assumptions can and do play such tricks with our thinking and acting behavior is, of course, well known. The feature we are stressing in the above "fixations" is their persistency, destructive or inhibitive of insight.

This phenomenon was not observed among chimpanzees, though it should be stated with regard to the comparative data on Failures that it is inadequate throughout, on account of Köhler's practice of frequently varying the situation after an initial failure. In this way or by means of clues, advisedly administered by Köhler but nevertheless unfortunately so for the purposes of this investigation, the solving process was often interfered with.

4. *Lack of Interest.*—This is often a chronic lack of enthusiasm on the part of the subject, causing him to "give up" too readily. Such an attitude is naturally not conducive to optimum or sustained attention, nor consequently to insight. Failure in seven

cases may be attributed to this cause. In experiments with animals this factor is efficiently counteracted by causing the animal to undergo a preparatory fast, by heightening the attractiveness of the objective, or, as was often done by Köhler, by introducing the competitive element. Though none of these devices was used for the subjects of this investigation, the situations themselves were found to be sufficiently compelling to arouse an active interest except in these seven cases.

5. *Discouragement.*—Three subjects were too easily distressed by failure. Sulks and tears, in any case a withdrawal of attention and cessation of activity, inevitably cut out the possibility of insight and hence of solution. Under similar circumstances the chimpanzee was whipped up to further action by introducing the competitive factor or by improving the objective. A verbal appeal was occasionally tried with the children, with only indifferent results.

6. *Excitability.*—When the solving process is too eager, or energetic or excitable, attention is not directed to any one thing at a time, with the result that excellent "clues" are often unheeded. It is an emotional state unfavorable to insight and is the cause of failure in seven cases.

7. *Lack of Observation.*—This is present in all degrees, from a total unawareness of surroundings, including the objective, to its extreme opposite, a minute investigation of all details. The extreme form of this inobservance is usually present only at the first exposure, due in part to a sudden change in surroundings, and gradually wears off to some extent. In two cases, however, this tentative, superficial, partly diffident attitude toward the changed surroundings was maintained through the five exposures, interfering with the arousal of insight. The chimpanzee, on the whole, has as strong a tendency toward exploration as has the child, but at times it, too, would "look without seeing."

8. *Emotional Immaturity.*—This, as described in Chapter III, presents a picture of inactivity, almost immobility. Under the circumstances insight is surely interfered with, if not completely inhibited. Failure in four cases can be attributed to this factor.

If, then, we are to classify Failure on the basis of insight we can say that it may occur when insight is absent, or when it is but vaguely present or when it is partially present, i.e., not extending over the whole situation, or when it is probably complete but not accepted or acted upon because of inhibitions. However, as we have seen in the foregoing analysis, failure can be expressed in terms of insight only if such an expression carries with it the conditioning factors of insight. These we have seen to be of a mental, emotional, and temperamental nature.

MISCELLANEOUS MODES OF BEHAVIOR

There are some bits of behavior which, though of slight significance in themselves, deserve mention here on the ground of their identical occurrence in apes and children. Thus, both apes and children will repeat a solution just to enjoy a newly discovered "stunt." The child either mounts the block several times after the actual solution to swing the objective again and again; or after procuring the objective, he throws it outside the pen to reach it again; or he will throw his hat outside and reach it as if it were the objective. And the ape, in spite of his hunger, will put off eating the banana he has already reached, and continue reaching for others and for pebbles when all the bananas are in; or he will try out the use of the block again and again after the first solution.

The child, as well as the ape, when unable to reach the objective outside the pen, will either throw something at it or will carefully push the stick out toward it, until it, too, is out of reach but in contact with the objective; he will derive considerable satisfaction from this contact, for he has in effect achieved a partial bridging of the gap between himself and the objective.

None of the so-called "foolish errors," those due to the perseveration of a solution, occurred in the solving process of children. This is not to be wholly explained by the mental superiority of children but partly by the fact that they were not made to repeat a solution while the apes were called upon to do so again and again, for demonstration purposes, or for other reasons, and by the further fact that sticks were not in sight during the block experiment and blocks were not in sight during the stick experiment; consequently, that the possibility of dragging the block to the bars in the stick experiment was ruled out. This was not the case in the chimpanzee experiments.

"Good errors," on the other hand, occur as commonly among children as among apes and are of the same general type. Thus in the stick-joining experiment, II-D, both apes and children, in an attempt to lengthen the stick, will hold on to both sticks placed end to end and attempt so to reach, as in Case 30, II-D, Chapter II. Structurally the stick is actually lengthened, but functionally not. Another instance of a "good error" is the attempt of Chica (an ape) to stick the box which proved too low a footstool, up against the wall on a level with her head, where she apparently hoped it would remain to receive her weight. This is not unlike the "way out" hit upon by the child, who, finding the block too low, ran over to a shelf, about five feet to the left of the objective from which it was as far out of reach in the horizontal plane as it had formerly been in the vertical plane. The child was just about to climb up when he checked himself and said forlornly, "Over there?" indicating the objective. (See Case 21, I-A, page 20.) The chimpanzee is also known frequently to check himself, as though on second thought. The use of a straw in lieu of a stick was another "good error" observed among children as well as among apes.

It is commonly believed that the validity of findings in human behavior is at least partially established if these can be found also among lower forms. It is therefore gratifying to find that the major conclusions of this investigation are as applicable to the solving behavior of apes as of children when both are confronted with the same type of problem-situation.

The differences pointed out in this section, such as the apparent absence of solutions with partial insight in the chimpanzee, the absence of delayed solutions among them, the greater dependence of the chimpanzee upon the physical juxtaposition of objective and tool in order to see their functional relationship, the well-nigh insurmountable difficulty which the problem of statics presents to the ape, the absence of those failures among them which seem to be due to emotional and temperamental factors,— these differences may be explained by the superior mental and emotional development of the child and by differences in technique.

CHAPTER VI

SUMMARY AND CONCLUSIONS

No attempt is made to summarize this investigation, for to do so adequately would require no less than a restatement of it, step by step as it was built up. In lieu of this, the following sections are presented by way of review: Quantitative Data, Conclusions, Practical Applications, and Suggestions for Further Research.

QUANTITATIVE DATA

Total number of possible solutions (see Table II-B).....248
Actual number of solutions (Table II-B)...179 or 72 per cent.
Total number of failures (Table II-B)......69 or 28 per cent.
Average number of exposures required to solve each problem-situation:

	Series I			Series II	
Situation	Av. No. of Exposures	Per Cent of Cases	Situation	Av. No. of Exposures	Per Cent of Cases
A	2.25	57	A	1.52	66
B	1.09	100	B	1.08	100
C	1.09	95	C	1.40	80
D	1.13	68	D	1.77	50
E	1.72	48			

Youngest subject reaching solution of Situation I-A, 23 months
Youngest subject reaching solution of Situation II-A,
24 months [1]
Oldest subject failing in Situation I-A............46 months
Oldest subject failing in Situation II-A..........49 months [2]
Correlation between mental ages and achievement on the present test-situations ....+0.266

[1] This is the youngest child used for this situation.
[2] This is the oldest child used for this investigation.

The low correlation of +0.266 can be partially if not wholly explained by the following facts:

1. The mental ages of preschool children as derived from the Stanford-Binet tests are not wholly reliable.

2. The scale which represents achievement on the present test-situations has been tentatively constructed and may not be wholly reliable.

3. The present test-situations allow a freer play of the non-intellectual factors, as self-consciousness, and the like, than do the Stanford-Binet tests, which factors, unless held in check by the experimenter, frequently interfere with the solution. It happens more often that high mental ages receive low scores than that low mental ages receive high scores, the ratio being 5 to 2.

4. Where children with low mental ages receive high scores, the discrepancy is probably to be accounted for by the keener participation of these subjects in the present test-situations than in the Stanford-Binet tests.

CONCLUSIONS

1. A child's solving activity was found to be determined more definitely by the nature of the problem-situation than by any one other factor. Thus, the same child will attack a problem in a random trial-and-error fashion or in a more deliberate exploration and elimination manner, depending upon the set-up of the problem. A semblance of confinement and a totally new or bewildering situation were found to stimulate the first type of response, while in the absence of these factors, the second type of response was the customary one. This is not to deny the fact that some children are more easily stimulated to the first type of response than others. The personal element functions here as elsewhere but not so potently as the situation itself. In its general statement this conclusion is equally true of apes.[3]

2. Exploration and Elimination was not only found to be the most frequent response but it also yielded the greatest number of solutions, alike for children and for apes.

3. No matter what the type of response, it culminates in a solution only if the subject has gained insight into the problem-situation. This, again, is equally true of both types of subjects.

[3] These conclusions, when applied to apes, are based upon Köhler's experiments reported in his book, *The Mentality of Apes.*

4. Though chance may aid the arousal of insight by throwing the elements of a situation into a suggestive constellation, no solution was found to be directly caused by chance.

5. It is also highly probable that insight is not always complete and stable before the solution, that is, that there are varying degrees of insight accompanying a solution; but no solution was found wholly unaccompanied by insight. There is no direct evidence that the first part of this conclusion applies to apes.

6. Transfer and retention seem to be indices not only of the presence of insight but also of the degree to which it is present. This needs to be further tested by an investigation specifically designed for the purpose.

7. The arousal of insight and its consummation in a practical solution are favored by emotional, temperamental, and mental factors—those which in effect constitute the total personality. This is true in a far lesser degree of apes, probably because of their lower level of development.

PRACTICAL APPLICATIONS

On the basis of the findings discussed in the foregoing pages, we submit the following recommendations for educational procedure with the preschool child:

1. Learning situations should be so formulated as to be interesting but not too stimulating, for the former type is more likely to arouse a solving approach conducive to the arousal of insight.

2. Analogous learning situations, where the greatest amount of transfer can be expected, are a useful check on the degree to which understanding or insight is present.

3. Retention of the principle learned in a given situation is another such check.

4. In view of the unstable nature of insight, especially when it matures after a prolonged struggle, it is wise to follow up the solution with one or more repetitions of the learning situation.

5. Some effort should be made with regard to self-conscious children to direct their attention specifically and actively upon the problem and away from themselves and the experimenter.

6. Children lacking in self-confidence and children over-reliant upon adult approval should be actively encouraged to try out all possible approaches to a problem.

For both types of children the important thing is to break up the paralysis which results from uneasiness and insecurity, an emotional state which is neither favorable to the arousal of insight nor to its natural consummation in a practical solution.

7. Children should be taught the habit of varying their solving procedure at a very young age. Such interference should, of course, be judiciously applied and only with those children who show a tendency toward unwarranted persistence at one aspect or feature of the problem. This persistence interferes with the seeing of the problem as a whole and hence with the arousal of insight.

8. Too frequent variation of the solving procedure is similarly to be discouraged, for it, too, interferes with the arousal of insight by the scattering of attention. Such solving habits are also wasteful of energy and usually compel an early cessation of activity due to fatigue or discouragement.

9. Children who show a tendency to become easily discouraged require an individual presentation of the problem where at least partial success is possible early in the period of endeavor. Discouragement at failure not only makes insight impossible in a particular situation, due to a lack of participation, but it tends also to color the approach to subsequent problems.

10. Children who lack a fair share of the tendency to explore should be frequently presented with situations which stimulate that tendency, for it greatly enhances the probabilities of arousing insight.

Though these recommendations are primarily for educational purposes, their applicability to the wider problem of mental hygiene is unmistakable. The test-situations used for this investigation furnish an excellent approach to a study of the individual as a whole, and the factors which were found to affect the arousal of insight are in effect those which constitute the total personality.

FURTHER RESEARCH SUGGESTED BY THE PRESENT INVESTIGATION

1. The Primary Criteria of insight as listed in Chapter III are those which constitute the solving attitude of the subject, whether tentative or assured. Though of a subjective nature, they are none the less of value and of a really specific nature. To use these data more objectively, it would be advisable to have several

observers compare notes on the total picture presented by a subject solving a problem-situation.

2. Retention and Transfer may be put to the test as secondary criteria of insight by comparing the degree of Retention of a solution after a given interval on the part of two equated groups, the one having solved spontaneously and with insight, as judged by the primary criteria and the other having been shown the solution after an initial failure. Similarly for transfer, results on situations subsequent to the key-situation would be compared for both groups.

3. The degree to which the presence of the experimenter stimulates the self-attentive attitude, thereby inhibiting the maturation and consummation of insight, can be readily tested by subjecting two equated groups to the same test-situations, one in the presence of the experimenter and the other with the experimenter seeing but not seen.

4. It is probable that Retention and Transfer are favored by spontaneous solutions more than by taught solutions, probably because of the fact that insight is more complete and stable in the former than in the latter case. This can be further tested by permitting the one of two equated groups to solve a key-situation spontaneously and the other to enact the solution only after a demonstration. The results of retention and transfer to subsequent situations are then to be compared for the two groups.

BIBLIOTHÈQUE CHAMPLAIN

3 9365 00156886 6